D0097663

OLD GLASS
Paperweights

OLD GLASS

Paperweights

THEIR ART, CONSTRUCTION, AND DISTINGUISHING FEATURES

BY EVANGELINE H. BERGSTROM

CROWN PUBLISHERS, INC.
NEW YORK

Fifth Printing, May, 1968

Printed in the United States of America

Dedicated to

MY HUSBAND, JOHN N. BERGSTROM

whose patience and fortitude
has assisted
the making of this collection
and the publication
of this book

FOREWORD

WHAT *are antique paperweights? Why do you collect them?" It is possible that Evangeline Bergstrom might once have found questions like these a trifle disconcerting. Not so today.*

Outside of a small circle of collectors, as Mrs. Bergstrom well knows, few people have had the opportunity to become acquainted with fine old paperweights, and it is probable that throughout the length and breadth of the land not more than one person in ten thousand is on speaking terms with the subject.

We are fortunate therefore to be permitted to view the glorious array of representative weights which Mrs. Bergstrom has brought together. Here are masterpieces from the French factories of St. Louis, Baccarat, and Clichy—outstanding for the lustrous softness of their glass, for the excellence of their workmanship, and for the fine artistic sense displayed in their exquisite designs. Here, too, are examples of the finest work of British and American glass workers; typical pieces from Venetian, Belgian and Bohemian sources; and a variety of odd pieces, each interesting for reasons peculiar to itself. We learn that the weights may be classified not only by the factories where they were made but according to subject and decorative treatments. Thus we have the millefiori weights, cameos or sulphides, and a great diversity of such subjects as flowers, fruits, snakes, and lizards.

One is struck by the fact that the makers of these

weights rarely repeated themselves. Resemblances may be noted between different treatments—just as there are similarities among paintings from the same school or the same brush—but nearly always the individuality of each weight is strongly marked. It would seem that each workman set out to produce a thing of which he could say, "There is in all the world no other weight like this."

Mrs. Bergstrom suggests in her book that one of the chief pleasures of collecting paperweights arises from the discoveries which are constantly being made. Since this is so, it would seem that there should be a fertile field for research among published and unpublished letters, memoirs, and factory records which might shed light on sources and original ownership. Who were the men who created these delightful fantasies in glass? Where did the workmen acquire their sense of pattern and composition? What events are memorialized in these lovely forms of crystal and color? What forgotten romances are celebrated here? What secrets remain hidden among the delicate traceries—and must these secrets be kept to the end of time?

Perhaps it is just as well that much of the story and romance behind some of the fine paperweights has been lost in the haze of time. Though the facts are gone, we still have the lovely forms over which we can exercise our imaginations, and from which we may be able to create poetry of our own. "Heard melodies are sweet, but those unheard are sweeter."

Mrs. Bergstrom has written a book which will be helpful to collectors of considerable experience, and yet it is one within the easy grasp of those who approach the subject for the first time. While it is intended primarily as a treatise on a little known form of art, it is something more besides. It is a "lure book" which may lead others to enjoy the rare pleasures which the author has found in this unusual field. It touches upon the methods of detecting the false and the true. It adds a page to industrial history, taking us back to "the elder days of art" when workers were proud and wrought with utmost care. It shows us that the gains made by modern mass production have not been all gain—that we have lost thereby some of the fine things which flowed from the old spirit of craftsmanship, and from the leisure which the best workmen earned under the factory methods prevailing in the second half of the last century.

HARRY J. OWENS

CONTENTS

OLD GLASS
Paperweights

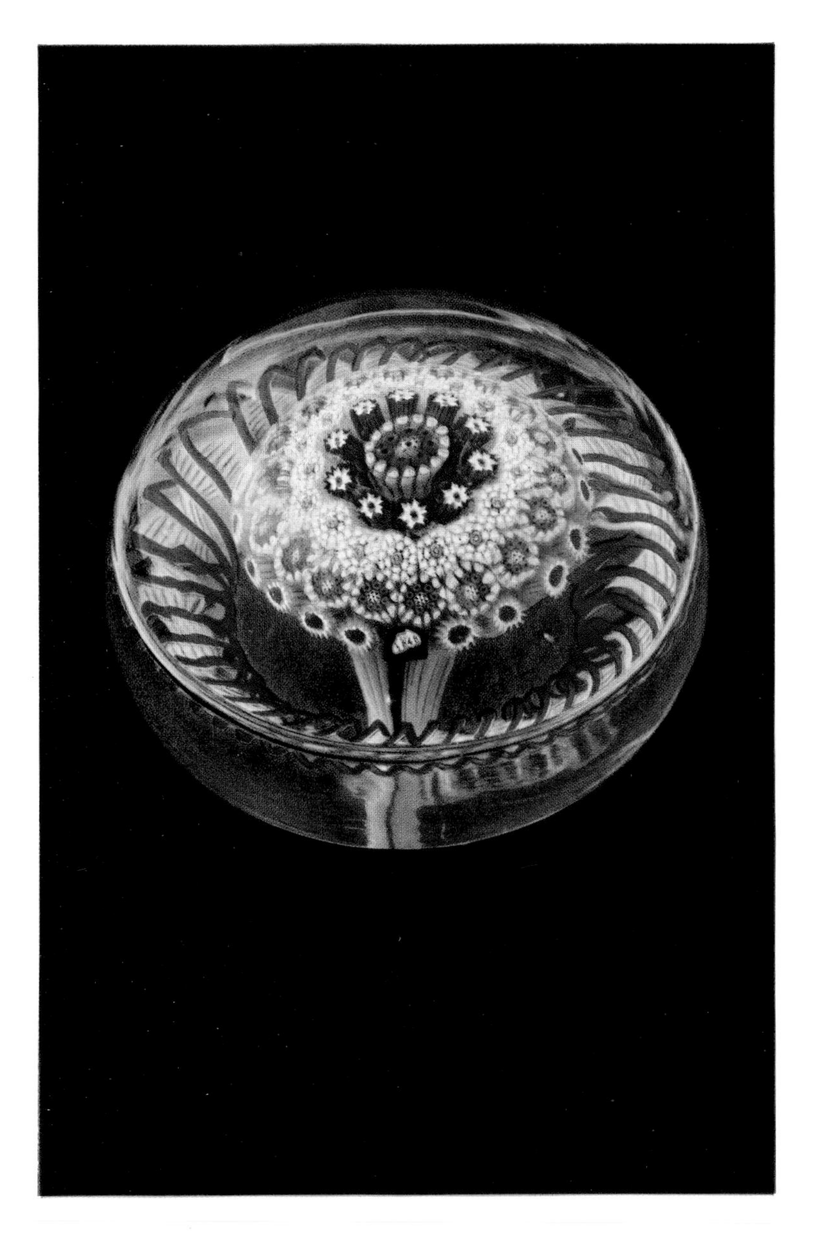

Plate II. *St. Louis*

hibits he will find in Egypt. In a tomb of one of the old Pharaohs near Thebes, for example, paintings on the walls show men blowing glass in very much the same way and with very much the same tools still employed in glass making at the present time. Still preserved is a glass piece found in the tomb of Thutmose II, who reigned about 1500 B.C.

Anyone who studies the old mosaic glass beads of the Egyptians will find in them the designs which served hundreds of years later to give workmen their ideas for the so-called "cane" patterns used in some of the early glass paperweights.

Many centuries later the art of glass making spread to Venice and Rome. In the 12th Century glass factories were so numerous in Venice that they became a fire hazard for the city. As a result, they were moved to the Island of Murano, where the secrets of the glass makers were guarded under penalty of death. Glass makers of those days ranked with the nobility, and a daughter of a count could marry a glass maker without losing caste.

1

Egyptian Beads

The story of Murano and its glass makers is found in a novel by Marion Crawford entitled "Marietta, a Maid of Venice."

At Altare, the seat of the glass makers' guild in the 13th Century, glass workers were eventually hired out to other districts—much to the distress of Murano. As a result, the art spread to Bohemia, France, and England; and centuries later, to the United States. There is no reference to Venetian glass manufacture before the 13th Century, although it is noteworthy that by this time St. Marks in Venice, built in 1159, had mosaics throughout its interior, and the Venetians of the 13th and 14th Centuries were already complete masters of the use of enamel.

II. HOW PAPERWEIGHTS WERE MADE

FOR the better appreciation of paperweights it is well to know something of the materials of which they were made, the tools and processes which entered into their construction, and the interesting niche which they occupy in the history of the glass industry.

The basic material of glass is lead or lime mixed with sand. The best glass is made by combining 40 to 60 parts of lead with 100 parts of pure sand. It seems almost incredible that these common substances, none of them transparent, can be fused to produce the marvelous quality and beauty of glass. Glass, unlike many other familiar materials, never loses any of its original substance and weight, and is therefore an excellent medium for preserving artistic expression.

Lead glass, often called flint glass, was invented in England in 1560. By 1676 it was used extensively in France, where it was called crystal, just as in America today. The word crystal is derived from a Greek word meaning "clear ice." Transparent quartz was called rock crystal because of an ancient belief that it was permanent ice which had been formed from water by intense cold.

Crystal is heavy, takes a brilliant finish, and constitutes the foundation of all old paperweights and cut glass. It comes out of the furnace red hot, like iron; and the "metal," as the molten glass is called, begins to change in its degree of ductility immediately. In the molten stage it is extremely tough and elastic, and readily lends itself to ladling, pouring, casting, and stirring. In the viscous state, it can be blown or rolled, and it remains plastic, ordinarily, for about three-quarters of an hour. It is generally transparent, but may be translucent or opaque. Generally speaking, high silica content in glass tends to make it hard, while high lead content tends to produce softness and luster. Glass has no grain, and, if a crack is desired, it can be pierced by a diamond cutter or a hot poker; otherwise it shatters under a sharp blow.

All the raw materials placed in the melting pot are called "the batch." The presence of too much iron or manganese in the sand impairs the clearness of the glass Metallic oxides introduced into "the batch" can be used to produce various colors, although the result will depend upon the nature of the mixture and may be modified both by temperature and the gases in the melting furnace. Copper oxide, for example, will produce green in a lead glass, and turquoise in a highly alkaline glass. Glass containing gold or copper looks red at lower temperatures, while with higher heat it may change to mulberry, and at the exploding point it takes on a soft lemon shade. The blue of cobalt, the chrome green or yellow of chromium, the violet of manganese, and the canary of uranium are all widely used. If oxide of copper is added to a mixture containing a strong reducing agent, a glass is produced which is colorless when it first comes from the crucible, but which, when reheated, develops a rich crimson or ruby color. Glass containing copper and gold behaves in much the same way, but with less intensity of the crimson effect. Cranberry red results from gold and copper mixed, oxblood from plain copper. Dark green can be produced from a mixture of copper scales and iron ore. Arsenic and antimony were used to secure the soft opaque enamel, sometimes called milk or opaque white, which we see on the overlay paperweights; also for the hard, opaque enamel which is found in the lacy set-ups and latticinio effects discussed elsewhere in this book—tin oxide and lead were used to provide a firm texture and a smooth surface to the mixture.

Not all factories made their own colored glass, but purchased it from others which specialized in that field. The result is a wide diversity in color, as well as in design, among the paperweights which came from widely different sources.

The old glass and the modern are quite different in texture. The old lacks the sharpness of the new, and it is said to have a softness to which the fingers of the expert are sensitive. It is probable that the glass "metal" was better in 1870 than today. True enough, the glass in some of the weights made at that time is uneven and has flaws, but it must be remembered in their favor that the workers of that period did not have the heating and chemical devices in use today. It may be remarked that some of the old weights show a swirl effect in the glass. This is explained, not, as some suppose, by inferiority of materials, but by the shaping and revolving motion to which the weights were subjected as they were fashioned. In any event, the fine design and execution of the old product stands in strong contrast to the inferior and crudely imitative character of many of the modern paperweights.

A furnace for melting glass material is technically called a *lehr*. It develops heat ranging from 600 to 1800 degrees. When the metal is thoroughly heated, a scum or glass *gall* forms on the surface. This must be skimmed off. The process of refining continues by bringing the metal to a higher degree of heat in order to eliminate all bubbles. It is then allowed to cool to a point where it is no longer a liquid but a viscous mass which can be gathered on a blow pipe and formed. Too long a period of heating sometimes gives the glass a yellowish cast.

Without attempting to cover the subject in all details, it will be apparent from the foregoing that many steps must be taken before the glass is ready for blowing, pressing, and casting, all of which require the use of molten glass. Another highly important step in the process of glass manufacturing is annealing, which is a systematic, gradual cooling to strengthen the product and make it resistant to the stresses and strains caused by changes of temperature. Because of the many separate elements which enter into the complicated structure of a glass paperweight, it is essential that all parts be annealed uniformly. Otherwise, damage or destruction will result from cracking.

A few more points are worth getting clearly in mind. Air bubbles in the glass are due to insufficient cooking of the metal. The tiny dewdrops on flowers and leaves, on the other hand, are produced deliberately with drops of alcohol. (See Illustration 2.) Unlike the finer small weights, large weights are easier to duplicate, and there is consequently more danger that any large weight is a modern duplication.

An impression prevails that the age of a paperweight can be determined by its faceting. In reality, differences are hard to discover—although it is true that a wedge-shaped wheel was invented about 1849 which gave a smoother and better appearance to the cut surfaces of some of the weights produced after that time.

Mention should be made of the special structural problems involved in the overlay weights. (These, it may be said in passing, are a joy to the collector and the finest examples of the weight makers' art—and they are constantly becoming more difficult to find.) After the

2

Sandwich

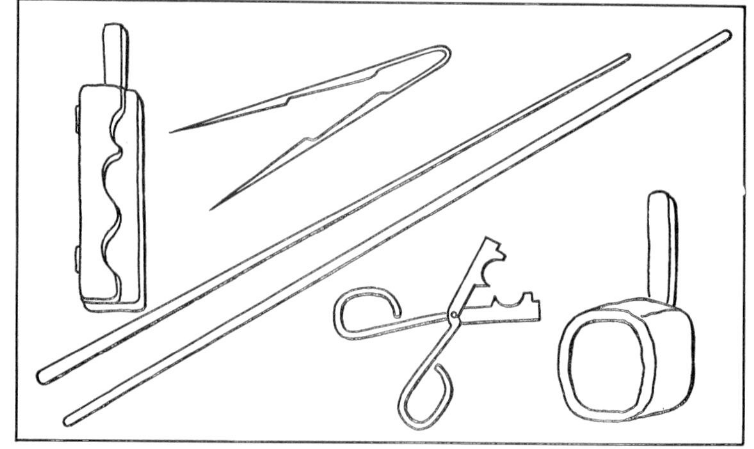

Drawn after photograph by Edmund W. Minns

Tools Used in Making Paperweights

overlay weight was all but finished, it was dipped in glass of another color, and the weight was then faceted to show the clear crystal and pattern underneath. A double overlay received two dippings—first in opaque white, then in another opaque color—before the facets were made. Most factories had their own special methods of cutting and faceting their weights. In an encrusted overlay weight, the color overlays and faceting were apparently followed by a final dip into clear crystal to complete the weight. Flash, an overlay color applied by firing, as in some of the Bohemian glass, is likely to wear off. It was never used on a fine old weight.

Although most weights were made by building rather than blowing, the *blow pipe* was an essential tool. This was a long, hollow metal tube with a wooden mouthpiece at one end and an expanded lip at the other. The size varied according to the article to be made. The *pontil rod* was an iron tool for holding the weight during construction. Other tools of the weight maker were *shears*, both sharp and dull; *tongs*, for picking up small objects; a wooden *spatula;* and a *marver*, or table, on which the glass was rolled to give it a symmetrical form. The marver was originally made of marble but later of iron.

The first step in making a weight was to take a thin piece of crystal or colored glass and decorate it as desired. It was essential that all the elements to be combined were brought to the same temperature. Otherwise the structure would crack and have the appearance of having been broken by a fall. Such cracks, however, would not be on the surface, but on the inside of the weight—around the pattern, like those which occur in many of Barber's first Jersey roses.

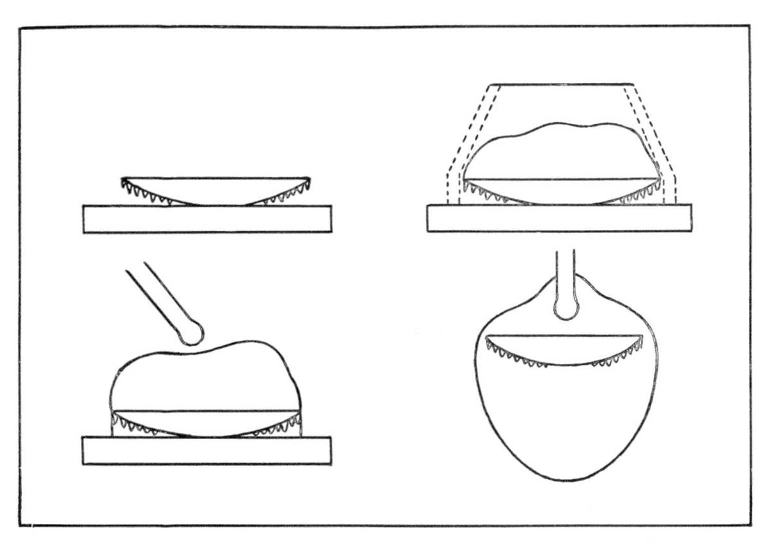

Paperweight Mold and Formation of the Weight

The decorated piece was then placed face down in a mold, which might be either flat or concave. It was then heated, a conical ring was placed over the mold and more glass was poured through the opening. This covered the back of the decoration. The ring was next removed and the pattern form taken up on the pontil rod. The decorated end was then dipped into more glass until it reached the form and size desired. At this point, the workman seated himself in a chair called a *cradle.* The cradle had large metal arms, and across them he rested the pontil rod, moving it quickly back and forth with his left hand, while a spatula held in his right hand shaped the mass to its proper size and form. As a final step, the weight was sometimes annealed in sand to produce a more brilliant finish.

A solid stick of glass, when plated layer upon layer, is called a *cane.* This was made in either of two ways. A workman following one method would gather a small quantity of glass on the end of a blow pipe and roll it on the marver into a pencil-like form. Next, he dipped this into a pot containing glass of another color. The dipping in various colors and rolling was repeated until he had a piece about five inches long and two inches wide. After reheating, an assistant attached another pontil rod to the other end of the glass, and the two workmen moved apart until the glass was brought down to the diameter desired. The consistency of the glass was such that patterns were undisturbed by the stretching.

By another method the patterns were formed in a mold. If the cane was to carry a figure—for example an animal, a four-leaf clover, a bird, or a butterfly—

a mold was made accordingly. The mold was then filled with the required amount of molten glass and allowed to cool to the proper degree. The cane was then removed, dipped and rolled to introduce as many colors as were desired, and finally drawn down to the proper size. Every cane was eventually cut into thin cross-sections by means of emery dipped in water, and the sections, called "set-ups," were carefully polished, and formed the attractive patterns in the weights.

In making the millefiori or mosaic set-ups (Ital. *mille,* "thousand"; *fiori,* "flowers"—"thousand flowers") the workmen took slender rods of different colors and fused them together while hot, welded them more firmly, and again drew them to the length desired. If a bubble appeared in any rod or cane, the same bubble was naturally repeated throughout its length.

In making a simple filigree, the workman took a quantity of crystal and put it into a long round mold lined with alternating opaque and clear crystal rods. This form came from the mold fused into a cylindrical solid. After marvering to perfect the amalgamation, it was heated again and given another plating of crystal. Then

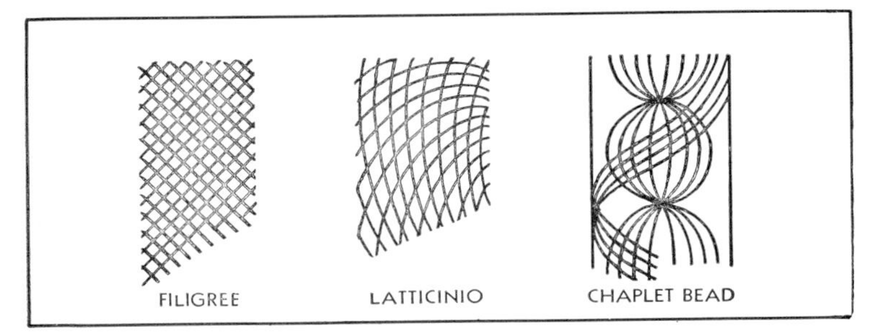

Basic Decorations for Backgrounds

a workman seated in a cradle took the free end of the glass in his pincers, and twirled the cylinder with his left hand, drawing out the spiral to about a quarter of an inch. Colored threads were sometimes added before the last plating to vary the lacy effect.

An unusual style of ornamentation is the lacy bead work. This is found in the early St. Louis weights. To produce this bead effect, six opaque rods were alternated with crystal rods in a cylinder. One end of the cylinder was sealed and flattened into a kind of sheath. More glass was gathered on each side of this structure, and the whole was molded into a cylindrical solid. Twirling in a complicated fashion transformed the imprisoned rods into the semblance of chaplet beads. Occasionally, red and blue threads of glass were added to this type of construction before the last plating of glass.

If the filigree was flattened while in the plastic condition, the Italians called it latticinio. To produce this effect, a delicate cylinder of glass was put into a clay mold which had been lined with alternating white opaque and white crystal rods. After their adhesion, these were removed from the mold and twirled to form a spiral pattern. A slight puff of air might be used to change the cylinder to a spherical form, and through the use of more heat, it could be collapsed like a hollow rubber ball. Fashioned to resemble lacy network, this filigree was given a slight plating of crystal to preserve its form.

Latticinio network had almost died out at the beginning of the last century, but it was revived during the period from 1830 to 1840. Latticinio effects often formed

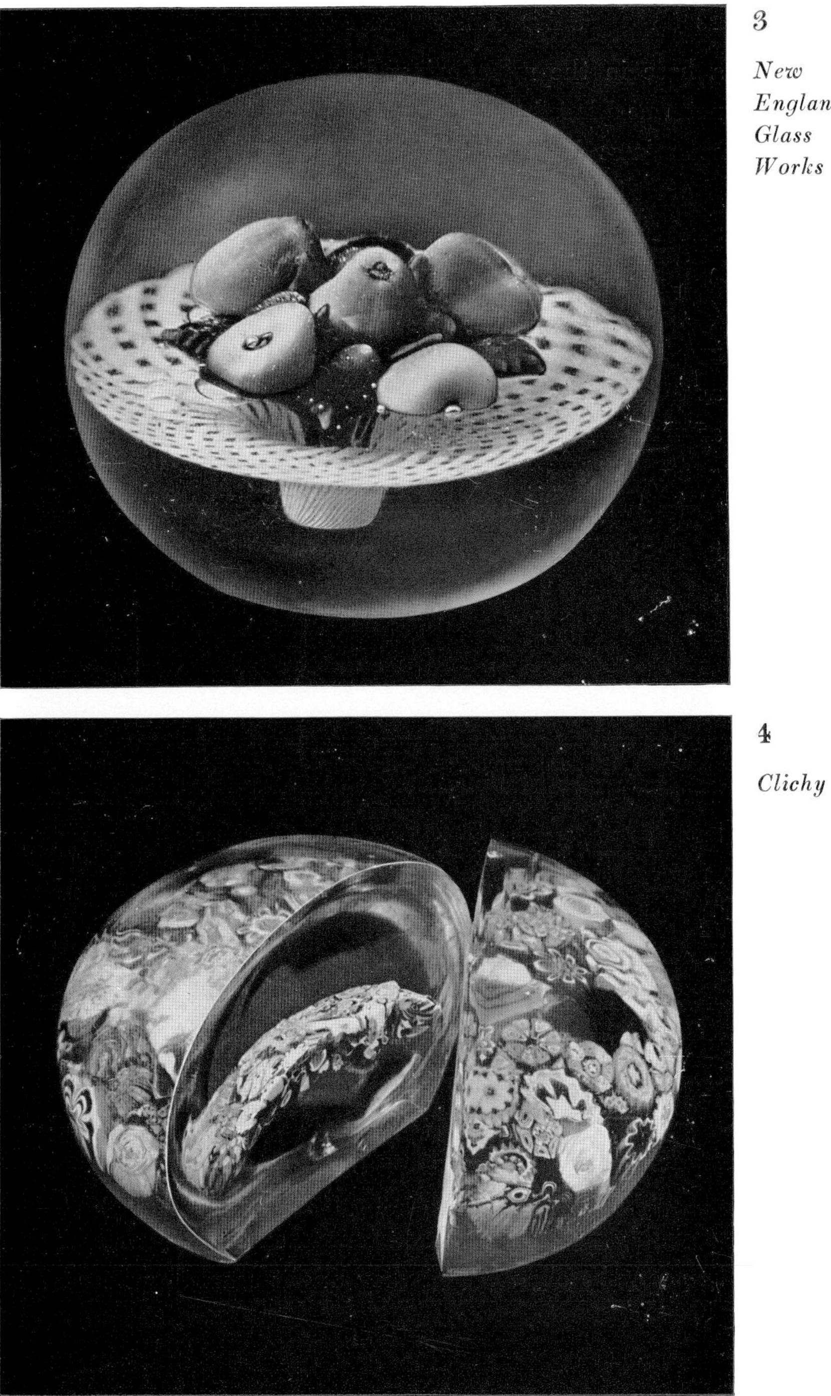

3

New England Glass Works

4

Clichy

a base in the millefiori and fruit weights. The delicate net was placed directly over the pattern in the weight, sometimes being separated by a thin sheet of crystal above the base. The skill lay in blowing to just the right size to fit the base of the weight. In the early fruit weights it was drawn to a point to give a basket effect. (See Illustration 3.) Heating and reheating were highly important, for it was necessary that everything be kept at uniform temperature to prevent cracking. Such pieces as fruits, flowers, and similar units were made and supported in crystal before they were applied. The petal, leaf, and stem of a rose, for example, were formed by hand, then assembled and surrounded with crystal. The veinings of the leaves were done by hand in the work room with a fine pointed instrument. The varieties of glass used had to be workable at various fusing temperatures, and they had to stand repeated heating.

In the great days of paperweight making, workmen were allowed to use for their own purposes the materials left over after the day's work. Moreover, if a workman of those times had completed his day's production—say, 300 glass tumblers—he was free to use the remainder of his time as he wished. Modern workmen do not have such free time, which undoubtedly explains why such arts as the making of the old paperweights have become extinct.

Now and then we encounter a weight of what is known as the "candy" type—a weight in which decorative odds and ends are arranged in hit or miss fashion. These probably reflect the old custom of saving all sorts of odd bits, on the chance that they might some day be used in paperweights. The cracked surface of the Clichy weight reproduced in Illustration 4 shows the thickness of the glass placed over the base and helps to explain the magnification which occurs when the weight is viewed from above. In the heyday of the art there was evidently some traffic in the canes and other semi-finished materials among the workmen, and it was sometimes necessary for the glass companies to prohibit their workmen from making paperweights in their spare time and entering into competition with their own factories.

Various cuttings are found on the bases of paperweights. In the small common star, which came into use about 1830, the cutting forms a complete circle. This replaced the pontil mark, which frequently left an unfinished appearance if not carefully smoothed off. The large star extending to the outside rim followed this. The flash star, which became popular around 1850, was divided into eight or twelve sections to form a star or a star within a star. The pattern star has points measured to the same radius, but forming a block diamond effect. This was used from 1890 to 1900. Clichy used the star, as well as the star and mitre cutting. The small diamond cutting appears both on the Clichy weights and those of Baccarat. The punty is found in many Baccarat weights—a concave cutting which *decreases* the apparent size of the pattern instead of giving it the usual magnification. This concave cutting in the weights sometimes served the purpose of a wafer glass.

Some subjects are used much more rarely than others. As anyone will have observed, who has studied any considerable number of paperweights, lizards are perhaps the most rare of all subjects; snakes next; and others follow approximately this descending order of rarity: millefiori, fruits, vegetables, butterflies, flowers.

The foregoing sketch of the methods used in making paperweights is presented less with the thought of absolute technical accuracy and completeness than to provide collectors with a fair understanding of the means and methods by which various results were accomplished. A weight turns up now and then which appears to fit into none of the usual identification patterns, but which, if it is well made, is nevertheless worth keeping; eventually, no doubt, more will be discovered of its origin and history. Much of the pleasure of collecting arises from the gradual growth of our knowledge of a subject which not so long ago emerged from almost complete obscurity. Half the pleasure of collecting paperweights resides in their endless diversity and the individual nature of the art which went to make them. The early weights are seldom duplicated. A workman almost never repeated a pattern exactly. He thought out his design after the day's work was finished, and his conception was doubtless elaborated throughout the process of creating it. In this modern day when the machine multiplies the same thing ten thousand or a million times, it is no little thing to reflect that the weight maker's art was not only original, but that almost every piece which came from his hand was unique.

Physically, there are six principal tests to which a paperweight should be subjected by the collector—

1. *Tint of the glass.* Make sure that it is not too yellow or uneven in its composition.

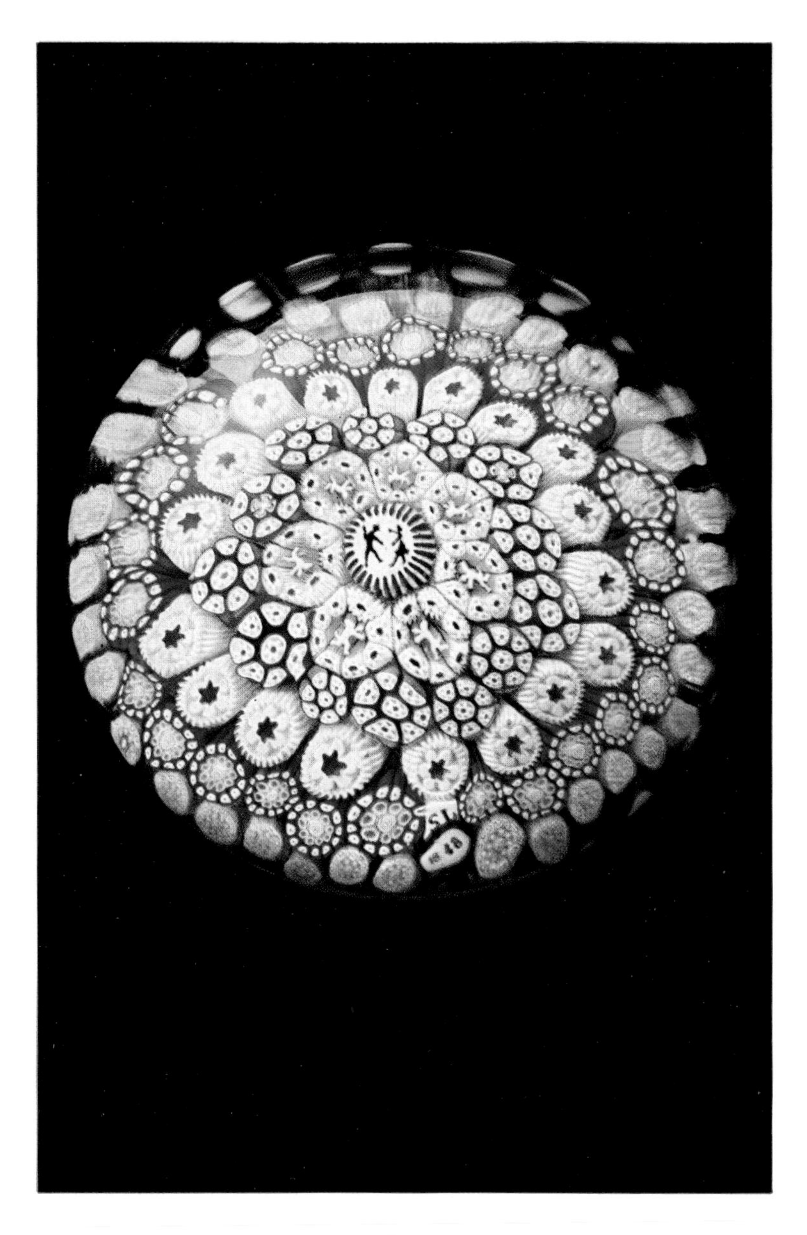

Plate III. *St. Louis*

PLATE IV. *Baccarat*

2. *Quality of the metal.* It should not contain too many bubbles or swirls.
3. *Weight.* How much lead does the metal contain?
4. *Signs of use or wear.* Fine old paperweights do not show scratches like those found on some modern weights which have been "aged" by rubbing the base on a stone.
5. *Pontil mark.* Roughness does not always indicate age. A good workman usually smoothed off the bottom of his weight to give it a finished appearance. The frosted base is *modern*—it never occurs on old weights.
6. *Workmanship.* See that the pattern is evenly applied, looks smooth across the top and bottom, and always extends to the outside edge of the base, with a well formed crown over all. If you are undecided between two flower weights, other things being equal, choose the one with a bud and nicely arranged leaves.

III. FRANCE

St. Louis

THE first fabrication of glass in France took place at Poitiers in the second century. The materials available in that locality produced a white glass with a peculiar greenish cast, and the few surviving specimens of the work of this primitive industry stand out as great rarities in the museums of France.

More than a thousand years may now be passed over at one bound to the 16th Century, when we find glass makers already established in the Vosges Mountains, a region destined to remain one of the famous centers for the manufacture of glass.

In 1782 La Verrerie de St. Louis was established by Henry Havard under the protection of Monsieur de Colbert and Louis XIV. St. Louis was located in these same Vosges Mountains, where sand of fine quality and fuel were both abundant. Fuel here means wood. As early as 1635 the English had found that coal fires, although they produced a glass of richer color, could not compete with wood fires in making white flint glass. Fine crystal required fires made from absolutely dry logs, cut into small pieces. Twelve hours of heating were necessary for forming the elements into clear crystal of the finest quality.

The first paperweights are supposed to have been made at St. Louis about the year 1820. Made from cullets and scraps, these were crude and rough—inferior in finish and appearance even to the "candy" type weights made in later years.

The first dated paperweights on which we have authentic information are those signed and dated "S. L. 1845." A small vase with a millefiori base, dated "S. L. 1845," but with the figures reversed, suggests that dates were unusual at that time. Very likely this was the first time the workman who made this vase had incorporated a date with the design, and the result was only partially successful.

The rose overlay *frontispiece* is a St. Louis weight of the mushroom type. The factory is firmly established by the canes in the mushroom.

The St. Louis weights of the millefiori and mushroom types were frequently signed "S. L.," and any weight bearing a signature or date is valuable. The name "St. Louis," it should be noted, was never spelled out in full. The date found most frequently is 1848, although 1847 is also known. In the mushroom type dated "S. L. 1848," the "S. L." is black, the "1" black, the "8" red, the "4" black, and the "8" red. These characters appear on a white surface encased in a black cane forming one of the outer parts of the design and extending to the center of the base (Plate III). The same composition is found in another type, except that the date is arranged among the canes appearing nearer the center. When "S. L." occurs without a date, the letters are shaded black against a cane with a white surface (Illustration 5).

St. Louis colors are softer than those of the Clichy and Baccarat weights. The wheel formation is characteristic of the St. Louis canes, and these wheels sometimes have a fine thread running from the outside rim. The dancing figures found in the canes of the St. Louis

5

St. Louis

6

St. Louis

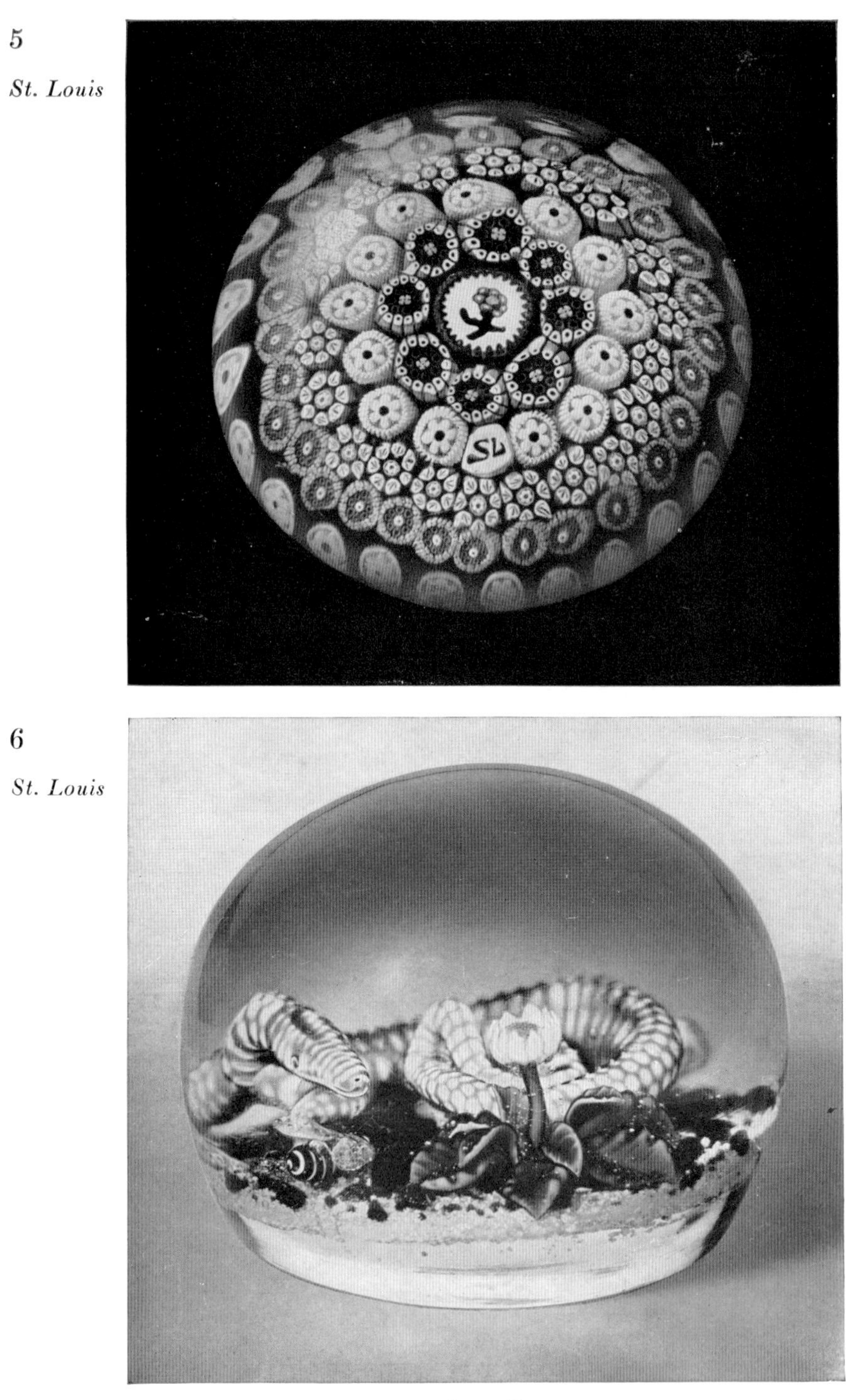

PLATE V. *Baccarat*

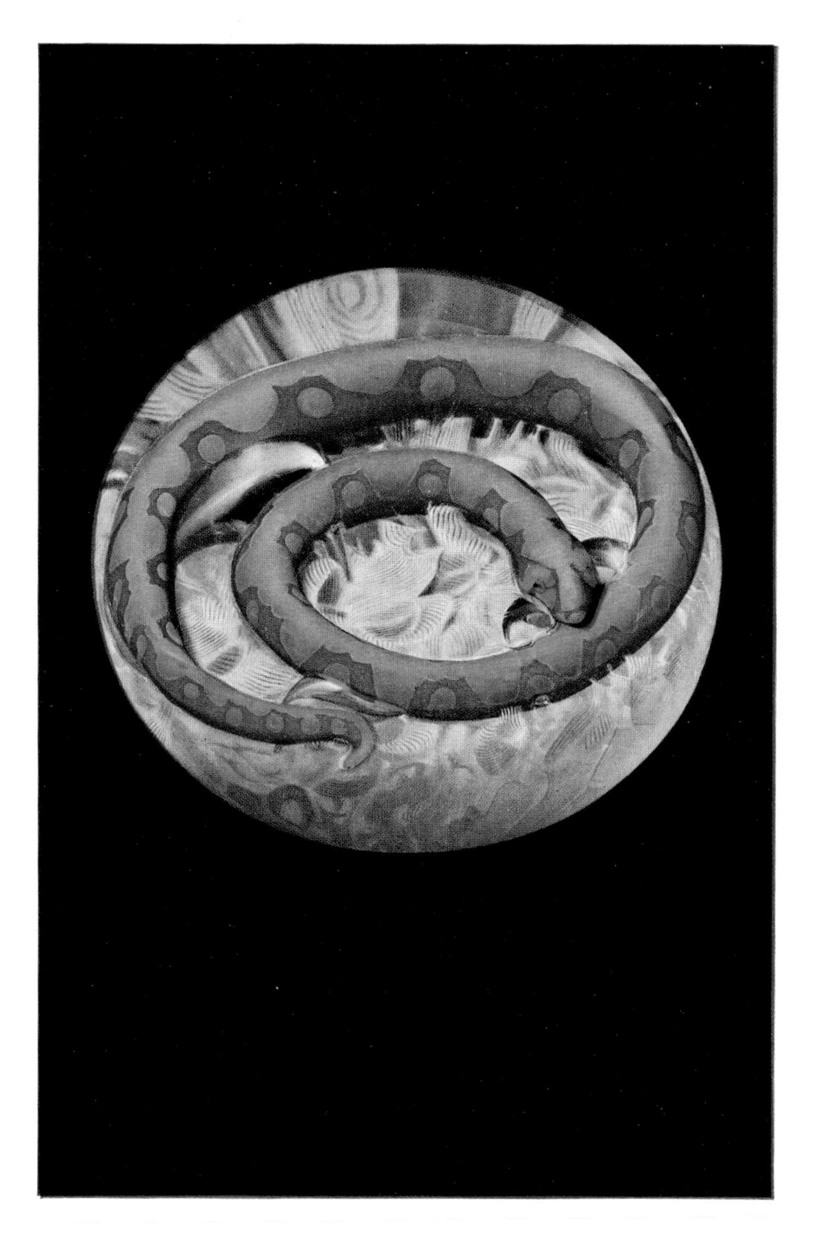

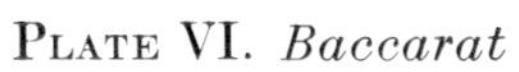

PLATE VI. *Baccarat*

7

St. Louis

weights are identifying features. The same is not true, however, of the monkey, camel or other animals, for these figures were used also in weights from other sources. The deep-well set-ups are individual St. Louis features.

The St. Louis factory seems to have been especially fond of the salamander or lizard, and one of the best of the old weights using this subject is shown in Illustration 6. The lizard in this case is represented as about to devour an insect on the ground. Another example, representing superb workmanship, is a hollow pink and opaque white overlay, and has a coiled salamander on the crown (Illustration 7). The deep blue entwining snake on a frosted base is another St. Louis creation—although the gold flecks, partially worn off, might seem

8

St. Louis

9

St. Louis

to indicate that it is a Bristol, for in the Bristol weights the gold often behaved in this manner. The St. Louis identification is established, however, by the bluish cast and hardness of the opaque base (Illustration 8). An especially interesting St. Louis is the "Ducks in the Pond" shown in Illustration 12. This weight stands out as a rare and important specimen. The little ducks are swimming in a clear glass pond, and green glass around the outside is intended to represent grass. Only a few of these weights were ever made. Among St. Louis flower subjects the favorite was the large full-blown aster, in pink, purple, or yellow. The asters used were sometimes so large that they covered nearly the entire base, scarcely

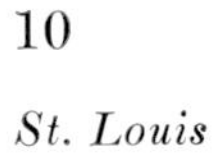

10

St. Louis

11

St. Louis

12

St. Louis

Courtesy of Arthur Kramer

leaving room for the points of a few green leaves (Illustration 9). In other weights the same flowers were used in smaller form, leaving room for a bud and foliage (Illustration 10). The leaves used in the St. Louis flower subjects are nicely veined, and the green is a shade lighter than that found in the Baccarat weights. The charming basket reproduced in Illustration 11, with its filigree spiral edge containing many colored flowers and green leaves, is identified as a St. Louis product through the wheel-shaped flower in the cluster. St. Louis workmen made the first crown weights. These were hollow, and they served not only as paperweights, but as bases for shot glasses, vases, and door knobs (Illustration 13).

13

St. Louis

A factory in France today still carries on the name of St. Louis, but it is not located on the old site and it is not descended from the famous enterprise founded in 1782. The original St. Louis establishment now operates as a branch of the Baccarat, having ended its independent existence in 1880.

Baccarat

Le Compagnie des Cristalleries de Baccarat was located, as the name indicates, in the little French town of Baccarat, in the Vosges Mountains about 150 miles from Paris. The factory was originally established under the name of le Verrerie de Ste. Anne in the year 1765. The first company went into bankruptcy, however, at the beginning of the 19th Century, and a high degree of success was not attained until the enterprise was taken over in 1822 by M. Goddard, whose descendants still carry on the business today. The proprietors of Baccarat looked far to the future: they rebuked workmen who failed to send their children to the school for craftsmen in glass, believing that the trade should pass from father to son, and that the highest skill and traditions could only be the product of more generations than one.

The Baccarat factory was the first to engage extensively in the manufacture of lead glass for windows and mirrors, and its colored glass was unsurpassed. This goes far to explain the fact that Baccarat paperweights rank first in quality, workmanship, and beauty of design. At the Baccarat factory, as at St. Louis, open pots over wood fires produced the superlatively clear, soft metal which contributes so much to the exquisite loveliness of the finest of the old paperweights.

The millefiori weights, supposedly originated in Venice about 1840, were made later in Bohemia, then at St. Louis and Clichy; but they attained their ultimate perfection at the hands of the workmen of Baccarat. The millefiori technique was also introduced into England, and weights of this type were in great demand in America from 1860 to 1880. Millefiori weights vary so widely in design, coloring, and size that it is easily possible to have a large collection entirely without duplications.

A Baccarat millefiori weight can always be identified positively if the canes are arranged over a lacy background and it is signed with a "B." This letter was at one time believed to stand for "Bristol," but this was an error which has long since been recognized. The Baccarat identifying signatures are often as follows, with a slight variation in color—

"B 1846" The capital letter "B" appears above the date. The "B" is red. The figures "1" and "4" are blue, and "8" and "6" are red.

"B 1847" The "B" is blue. The figure "1" is green, "8" and "7" are blue, and "4" is red.

"B 1848" The "B" is blue, "1" and "4" are green, and "8" is red in both uses.

"1849" So far as known the letter never appears over the date. The figures "1" and "4" are green, and "8" and "9" are red.

The dates 1847 and 1848 are most common in the Baccarat weights. Even if the weight is not dated, however, you may be sure that it is a Baccarat if you find

14

Baccarat

15

Baccarat

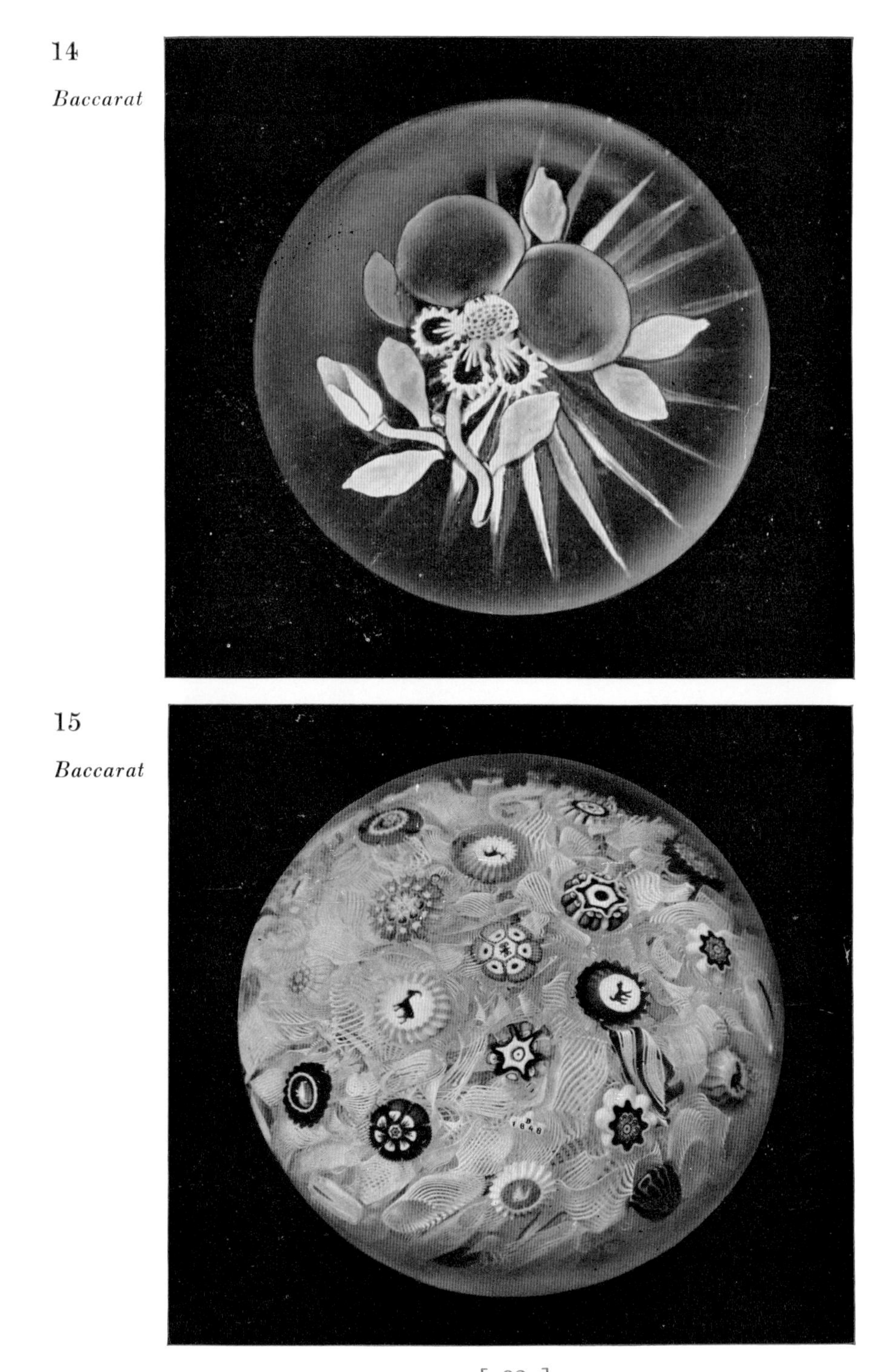

PLATE VII. *Clichy*

PLATE VIII. *Clichy*

in it a honeycomb or similar cane. The star-shaped set-ups within the Baccarat canes are most characteristic, and they frequently serve as backgrounds for the larger canes in the weight, as well as for the centers of flowers such as pansies or dahlias. The Baccarat pansy is easily distinguishable from that of any other factory. It has two very large, deep-purple petals and three small dark blue petals having a white heavily fluted outside rim and white veining. The honeycomb set-up always marks the center and serves to set the Baccarat product clearly apart from that of any other factory. (See Illustration 14).

The Baccarat weights shown in Illustrations 15 and 16 are similar in design to the Clichy weights shown in Illustrations 25 and 26. The signatures are always found slightly to one side of the design, never in the center. Other devices which are familiar in the Baccarat weights are the maltese cross, and canes whose cross sections carry minute images of animals, birds, and butterflies. Baccarat compositions included a wide range of subjects and a greater variety of patterns than any other factory.

Especially deserving of attention are the Baccarat overlay weights. They began to cut overlay weights about 1870. The surface coatings of colored glass which are called overlays were applied in many colors. In the single overlay, the colors used most frequently are red, dark blue, and green (Plate IV). In the double overlay weights, light and dark blue, rose and occasionally emerald green are found in both the mushroom type and in the weights containing various circle set-up arrange-

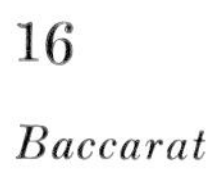

16

Baccarat

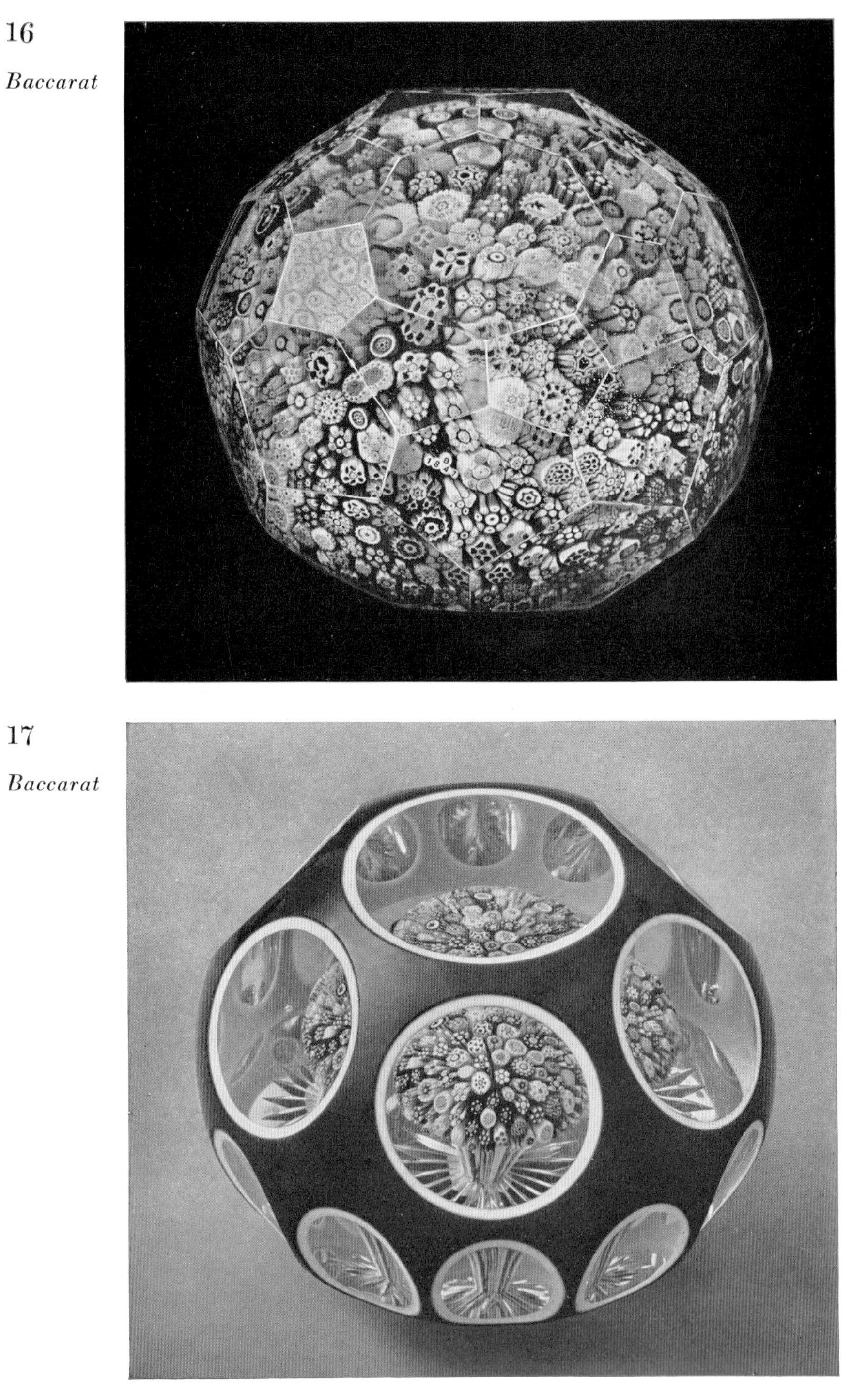

17

Baccarat

ments (Illustration 17). The Baccarat factory was the only one which made paperweights in the encrusted overlay style (Plate XV).

Among the many fine Baccarat weights, the fruit and vegetable subjects have an individuality which is especially pleasing to most collectors. After lavishing one's affection for a time upon the weights built upon abstract patterns, it is gratifying to turn to a subject that is extremely simple—a tiny decorative basket, for example, filled with flowers that will never fade; or a cluster of cherries, cool and juicy looking against a background of bright green leaves (Illustration 19); or the delicate radiance of a butterfly that has alighted on a summer flower (Plate V). These simple subjects also include dahlias in shades of white, pink and yellow, often with a bud and leaves (Illustration 20). Frequently the crowns enclosing some of the finest of the weights in this group are faceted, and the facets interpose a serious obstacle when an attempt is made to secure adequate photographs.

Discoveries are constantly being made in the field of Baccarat weights—and, for that matter, throughout the entire realm of paperweights. Collectors have been accustomed, for example, to look for the "B" over the date in all 1848 millefiori weights, but recently one was found in which the "B" occupied the center of a cane slightly removed from the date. Some day—who knows? —a yellow overlay may turn up to startle collectors. It is certain that much interesting information remains to be uncovered, although it scarcely seems likely that much will ever be known of the individual artists who

18

Baccarat Vegetable

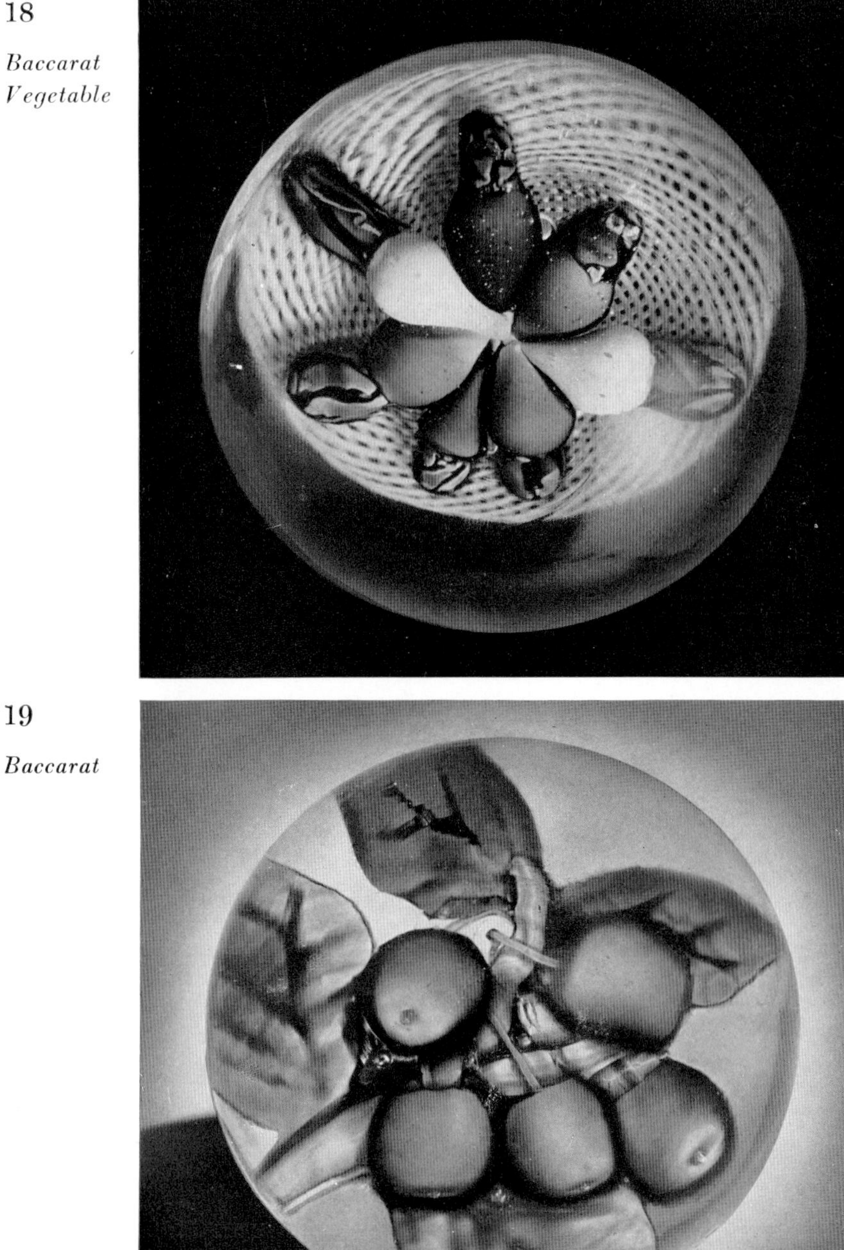

19

Baccarat

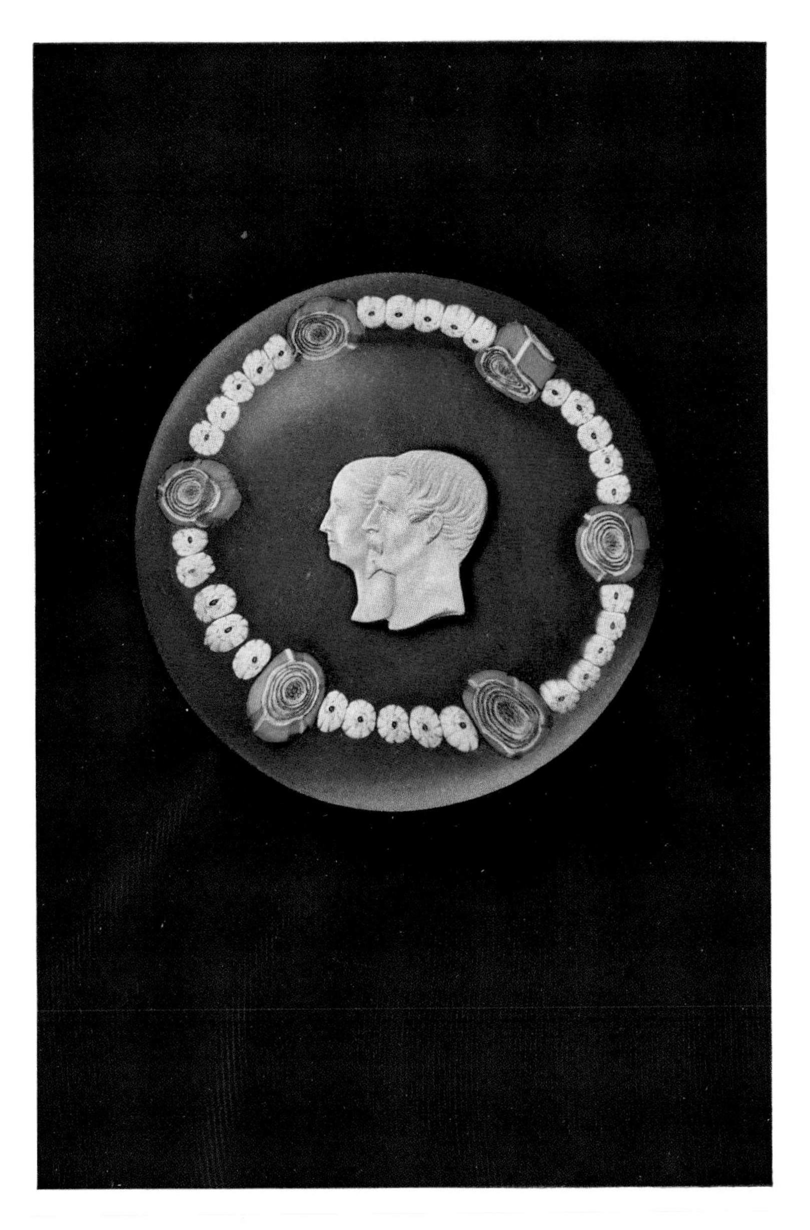

PLATE IX. *Clichy*

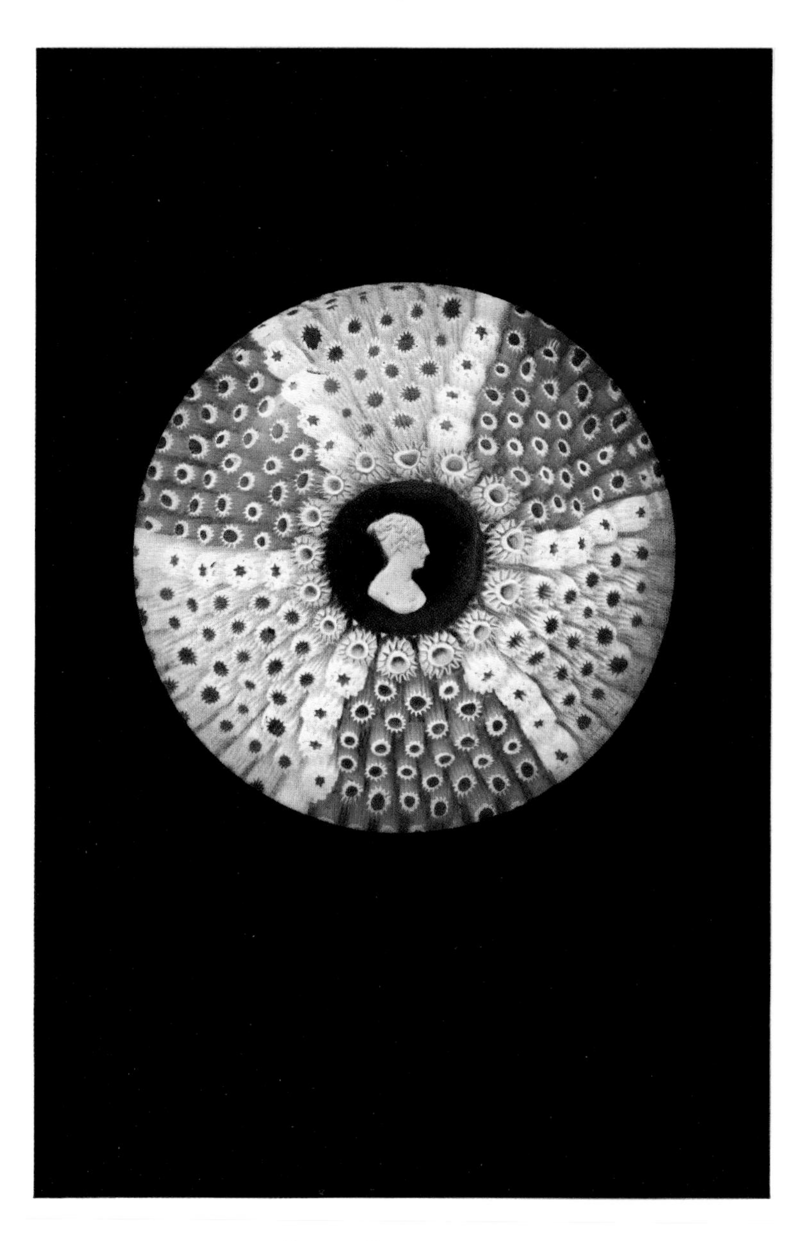

PLATE X. *St. Louis*

produced the fine old weights, or of the "story" which doubtless lay behind many of their creations.

Anyone who lives with a fine collection of paperweights, however, is constantly tempted to speculate upon their possible history. This fine Baccarat, for instance, with its cross of leaves, its passion flower center—how did it come into existence? Was this perhaps the kind of poetry used by a young workman to express his wishes for a Happy Easter to his mother and father? Whatever the sentiment or the circumstances, it is sure that this glass-artist was a man of fine sensibilities, of surpassing skill, and of such integrity that no detail, however minute, suffered by neglect. So far as he was concerned, "the gods see everywhere." (See Illustration 21.)

But, to return to the subject of the Baccarat factory and its products, it may be well to set down a number of miscellaneous points which may be of some interest.

If signed and unsigned weights are examined carefully, identical patterns may be discovered which will establish their relationship. Unsigned weights may in this way prove their right to the Baccarat classification.

All old millefiori weights, whether Venetian, French, English, or American, are interesting. Modern weights of this type from Czechoslovakia and Japan, however, must be eliminated from serious consideration by the collector. These can be identified easily through the fact that their crowns are usually higher than those of old weights of the same size. Moreover, their set-ups are not cut evenly, and usually extend below the design.

20

Baccarat

21

Baccarat

BACCARAT ST. LOUIS

ST. LOUIS

Courtesy of Mrs. J. H. Sinclair

BACCARAT

22

Ladies' Hand-coolers

When looked at crosswise, the design appears uneven and it never has the perfection of arrangement found in a fine antique weight.

In the Baccarat snake compositions a sandy effect for groundwork was sometimes mixed with green for undergrowth. A large weight might, for example, represent the earth of the Mesozoic Age. In one fine specimen of this type three green plants with white and red blossoms rise from a sandy base in green and buff. In the center of the weight stands a black animal with a long white-spotted tail, the ferocity of the beast confirmed by its balefully glowing red eye. This weight is an outstanding example of its kind. The snakes with raised heads are considered superior examples. The one shown has red and green markings and rests on a lacy background which was also used. (Plate VI).

Baccarat, as well as many other factories, produced the egg-shaped pieces of glass which were known as "ladies' hand-coolers." (Illustration 22.) According to tradition, these were originally devised for fair ladies in the days when hand-kissing was in fashion. The lady simply held the glass in the palm of her hand until the time came for the ceremony, whereupon the gallant was pleasantly surprised to find the hand cool and comfortable to the lips. If products of this sort were offered for sale today, one can easily imagine what modern advertisers would make of them! The aura of romance which surrounds the "hand coolers" is at least partially dispelled, however, when we learn that they were made by most factories from cullets, and that they frequently served as stocking darners.

Glass paperweights served as bases for a variety of articles useful in their day—many of them made by Baccarat as well as other factories. The wafer glass held the wax wafers used in sealing letters. Shot or sand glasses were used for holding long quill pens. Pedestals

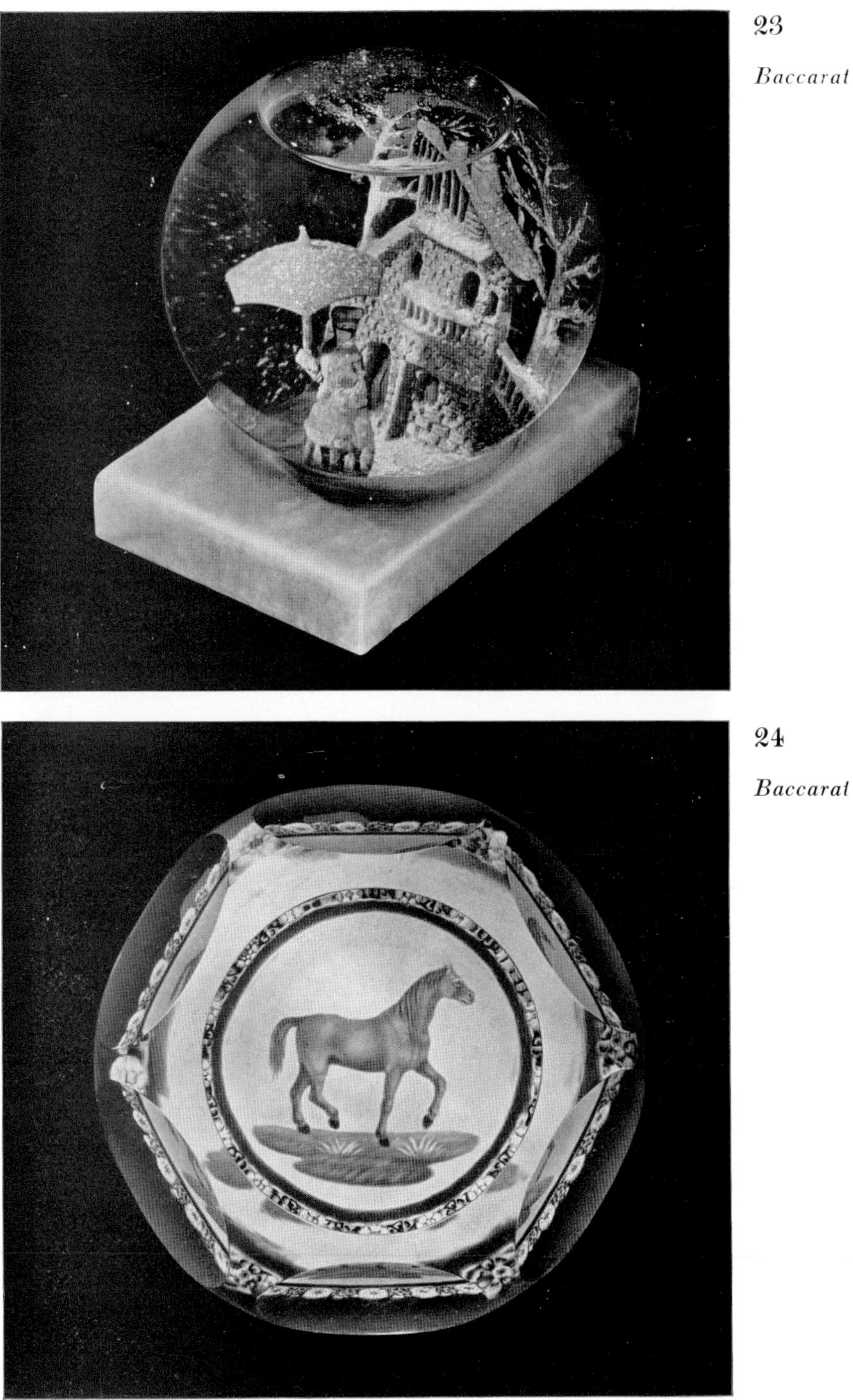

23

Baccarat

24

Baccarat

1. Cologne Bottle, *St. Louis.* 2. Witch Ball, or Seine Float, *Nailsea.* 3. Mantel Ornaments, *Bristol.* 4. Shot Glass Pen Holder, *St. Louis.* 5. Ink Stand, *White Friars.* 6. Wine Glasses, *Baccarat.* 7. Wine Glass, *Sandwich.* 8. Wig Stand, *Baccarat.* 9. Vase, *St. Louis.* 10. Powder Box, *Baccarat.* 11. Toasting Glass, *Bristol.* 12. Newel Post, *Clichy.* 13. Wafer Glass, *Clichy.* 14. Vase, dated 1845, *St. Louis.* 15. Wafer Glass, *Baccarat.* 16. Shot Glass Pen Holder, *Baccarat.* 17. Witch Ball, *Nailsea.* 18. Table Ornament, *Millville.*

to hold wigs, ink bottles, vases, mantel ornaments, door knobs, door stops, and newel posts—all of these were frequently embellished after the manner of the old paper-weights, or weights were incorporated in them in one way or another.

All the snow weights were French. The snow and the liquid which they contained were made by a chemical formula which has not been duplicated in modern times. The old weights of this type were mounted on bases of china or marble. Those made today are usually mounted on bases of wood or some composition material. One of the finest of the old snow weights contained a green tree spreading over a diminutive castle. The castle forming the background was made of a brownish, rubber-like material which has the strange property that if it is exposed to a high temperature it will bend out of shape and cannot thereafter be restored to its former position. The snow weight shown in Illustration 23 has in the foreground a woman dressed in red and carrying a red parasol. Red predominates in the dress of many of the figures in weights of this kind, and it may be said in general that red was a popular color in the design of most of the old snow paperweights. These weights were made about 1850, and it is held by some that they were intended primarily as toys for children.

The Baccarat factory is not only in existence today, but it is still one of the finest glass manufacturing establishments in France. It is to be regretted that its workmen no longer produce the exquisite little creations which are enough in themselves to shed glory upon the name of Baccarat forever.

25

Clichy

26

Millefiori Clichy

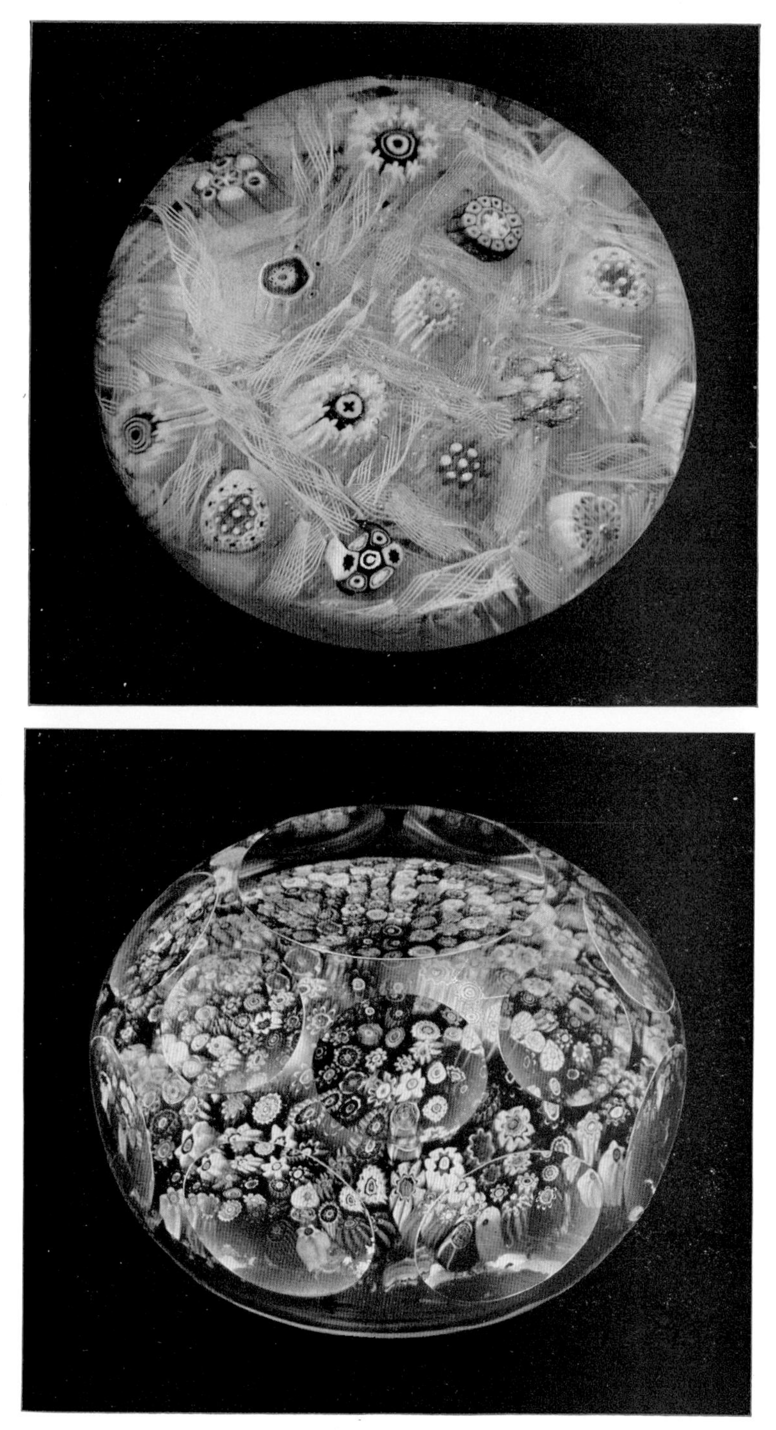

Clichy (Clichy-la-Garenne)

The old city of Clichy, the seat of kings in the 11th and 12th centuries, later a suburb of Paris, and finally an industrial center, became the site of what was probably the second factory in France to make glass paperweights. The same vein of pure sand which extends from St. Louis to Baccarat and Fontainebleau is found at Clichy. Although little of the history of this factory has been recorded, we do know that it was founded in 1840 and that its business was finally liquidated in 1870.

It made some ordinary bottles but also many beautiful ones of the overlay type, as well as decanters, jugs and tumblers, which followed the Venetian type of cutting and engraving.

A Clichy paperweight can easily be distinguished if it has a pink or white rose incorporated somewhere in its pattern. This was an individual factory symbol. The use of this rose may have been inspired by the Jacobites, who used a glass ornamented with a white rose when drinking a toast to the Pretender. A purple rose and an open purple flower are color variations not often seen, but they are found occasionally in a wreath or cluster formation of flowers in Clichy weights (Illustration 27).

Most of the canes in Clichy weights are of opaque colored glass, with a decided flare at the base. Many of these are inserted in a brightly colored opaque background of rose, green, purple, or white (Plate VII). In the Clichy millefiori weights the canes are arranged on a crystal background, and nearly always a Clichy rose

27

Clichy

28

Clichy

is found somewhere among the canes. The canes arranged on a lacy background are similar to the Baccarat.

Some Clichy weights were signed with a capital "C" in black, green, or red in the center of a cane, but few were ever dated. The name Clichy has also been found in some specimens in very fine letters, but this is extremely rare. Even Clichy weights of the "candy" type, a generally inferior type of weight, were sometimes signed with a "C," and in the canes are to be found bits of a Clichy rose.

The pear weight shown in Plate XI is typical of the Clichy fruit weights. It will be noted that the background in this case consists of an arrangement of straight lacy canes. Another signed specimen from this group shows the canes set in squares of lacy filigree (Illustration 25).

The Clichy overlay weights are of the double overlay type. The opaque glass forming the outside overlay is usually of light or dark blue, rose, or a green, which is very rare, and the center canes are often arranged in the mushroom style and usually contain a Clichy rose. The faceting of the circles is smaller than found in the St. Louis weights, and a single overlay has yet to be found. All the French factories made a mushroom type of weight. The Clichy snake weights are interesting and easily distinguishable from those of Baccarat. The Baccarat snake subjects are usually placed upon a sandy background. Clichy weights of this type, on the contrary, were formed upon a lacy background. The swirl weight comes in all the colors of the Clichy factory and the characteristic canes appear in the center unit (Illustration 28).

29

Baccarat

30

French

The construction of glass paperweights in general, and of a signed Clichy candy type weight in particular, is brought out by the illustration of a cracked section shown in Illustration 4. The picture shows clearly the depth of the canes used in forming the pattern.

The Clichy glass paperweights which are the subject of this chapter should not be confused with the Clichy glass prints. These glass prints had a great vogue in France during the Renaissance, but they were not made at the Clichy factory. The characteristic "scratches on glass" were made through exposure of the prints to the sun. The process was used by Corot, Daubigny, Millet, and Rosseau. It is one that is entirely forgotten today,

31

Clichy

but it is often mistaken for glass made at the Clichy factory.

The collector of antique crystal will do well to bear in mind that there were no schools for glass such as there were for porcelains like those produced by Wedgewood or Haviland. In glass, everything is much more vague and indefinite. It must be recognized that in assigning certain items to certain classes, the classification is often based upon nothing more substantial than a supposition. Collectors have no other choice but to bide their time in the hope of learning more eventually regarding some of the French compositions.

A word about some of the other subjects chosen for illustration. The beautiful yellow rose on a deep blue background shown in Plate XVII has a third dimension not found in the products of any other French factory mentioned. The attractive daisy (Illustration 30) is likewise unique, for the construction of its center does not resemble that of the known makers. Either or both of these weights may have been made by St. Gobain or Escalier de Cristal. The probability seems to favor the second name, which was well known for its excellent medallions.

Little or nothing is known about the other fine factories in France whose workmen undoubtedly produced paperweights. Few records were kept. Often fine paperweights were masterpieces that glass makers produced when they were through with their mastercraft exams —"Maître Ouvrier." The weights were made at odd hours for friends or valued clients whom the manufacturer wished to honor with unusual and individual gifts. Even a trip devoted to exploration and research in France might not prove particularly fruitful, for such effort, because of the unfortunate lack of records, has not been especially rewarding here in America. The old Corning factory, for example, produced some of the finest of the American paperweights, including the beautiful Corning magnolia. Yet, until this weight was brought to its attention, the modern Corning management was not aware of its existence.

Cameos or Sulphides

Sulphides, as the French term them, constitute a class by themselves. Major Enperauger, in a pamphlet published in 1909, describes them as encrusted cameos and crystal medallions. They have a rich history.

The art of encrusted glass came from Bohemia in the 13th Century. It was completely lost for a time, but was revived in France and England at the end of the 18th Century in the form of cameo under glass. In the early days of the art, the Bohemians had used small figures of grayish clay in their encrustations, but the result was not successful for the reason that the glass and clay did not adhere to each other equally. The process was next taken up and improved greatly by the French, who sold their product at an extremely high price. The vogue of the sulphides continued in France until the reign of Napoleon III.

It has been said that the original idea for the sulphides resulted from the silvery appearance of drops of dew on flowers. Experimenters found this beautiful silvery effect could be secured through combining fine white china clay with crystal. The clay had an unpolished body and could be made to withstand a higher temperature than the crystal. The silvery effect which resulted from this combination led to the name "sulphides" (of silver) or "nitrates" (of silver).

Sulphides were immensely popular in their day. They were used on many articles made of glass, such as goblets, flasks, vases, and boxes. They were encased in flat surfaces of cut crystal, as well as in the oval forms found in paperweights. Important pieces were inscribed with the names or initials of the sculptors.

In France a colored opaque or clear glass base was frequently used in the paperweights, and upon this the encrusted figure was superimposed. The enclosing glass was always the finest crystal.

The sulphides took many forms. The subjects included medallions of celebrated people, religious or allegorical medallions, and seals like that of the Legion of Honor. Three sulphides showing Napoleon I and Marie Louise in profile together, and one of them showing the Imperial couple with their son—all made by Andrieu—are most valuable. All of the sulphides made by Andrieu represent Napoleon with a laurel crown; while those made by Galle, without the crown, are very rare. Emil Galle, who died in 1904, had a school at Nancy, France, in 1846, where he taught the process of encrustation.

In making cameos, a wooden mold was first carved and then cast in iron. A ceramic composition was poured into this sliding iron mold, slightly baked, and gradually cooled. When the cameos were required for encrustation,

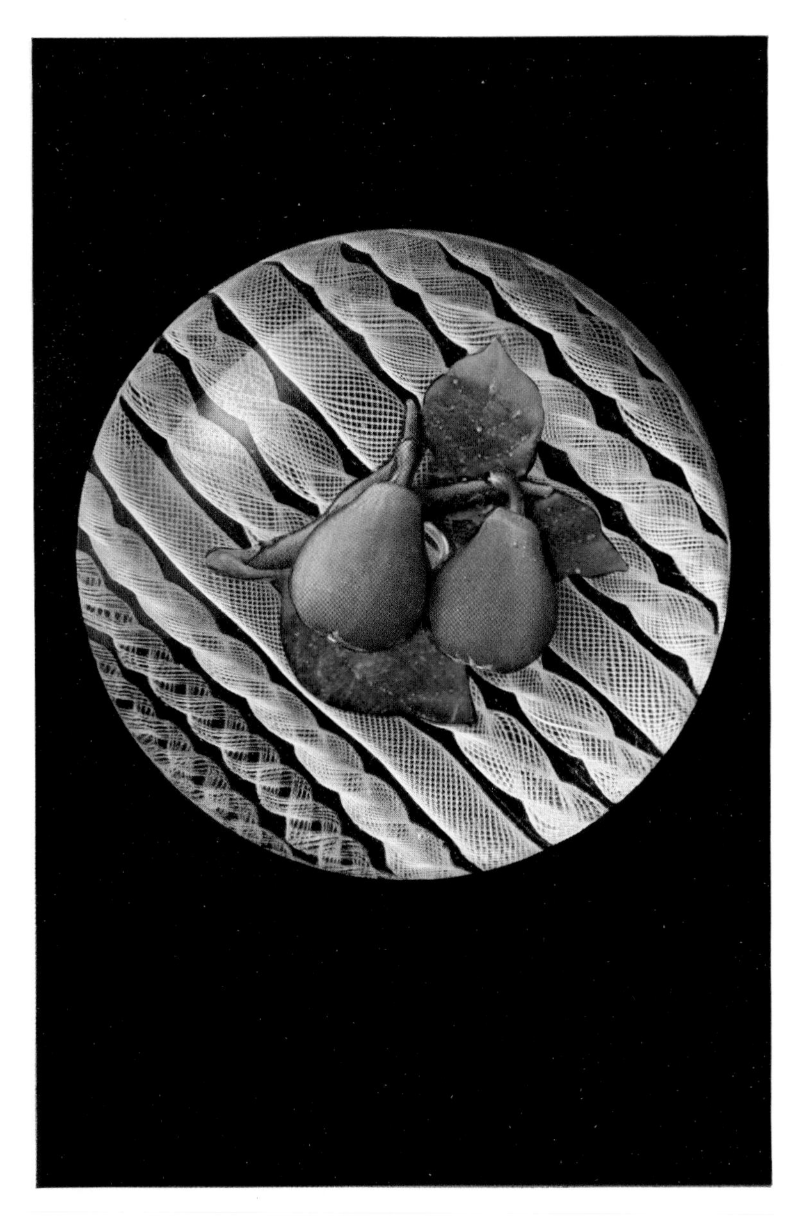

PLATE XI. *Clichy*

PLATE XII. *Baccarat*

32

Baccarat. Signed by the artist, Andrieu

33

Bohemian. Charles X

they were reheated to a red state in a small oven made for the purpose. Properly cooled, they were carefully removed and centered on a glass base of the same temperature to prevent cracking, and the process that followed was the same as in the composition of other paperweights.

34

Imperial crest engraved on bottom of weight, Plate IX

The molds were always cleaned by men who did nothing else. If the slightest imperfection appeared, the molds were cast aside; it was impossible to repair them successfully. As may be surmised, the unequal density of clay and glass resulted in a high percentage of breakage. Consequently, there are few duplications among the sulphides.

In Pascal Greppe's article on sulphides, he pictures twelve encrusted cameos of Napoleon I in right or left profiles, or full face. The one of Napoleon I with the guiding star is by Andrieu (Illustration 32). In this weight the cameo is placed on a light blue surface which was made at the Baccarat factory. The one picturing Napoleon III and Eugénie was a product of the Clichy factory. It is readily identified by the rose, and was evidently made for the Imperial family, since it has the Imperial crest engraved upon the base (Plate IX). The full length portrait of Napoleon I on a deep blue background has the large green and small red canes which are characteristic of many Clichy weights (Plate VIII). The one of Josephine is as fine as any jewel, and, from the canes and patterns in this weight, we know it came from the St. Louis factory (Plate X). Those of Queen Victoria and Prince Albert, each on an amber background, are very rare, and were supposedly made by Apsley Pellat. Those on a black background are also very scarce. Many of the fine French cameos were made by a man named Pazaurek.

Another sulphide picturing Charles X came from the collection of the Marquis de Baillou, Château d'Angerville, and was probably made in Bohemia; for the medallion placed on a protruding clear ruby base, is accompanied by a vine pattern in gold around the rim and sides, and also has the enameled decorations characteristic of Bohemian glass. It is extremely heavy, and has a deep star-cut base which extends to the outside rim of the weight. The cutting, moreover, has a different feel-

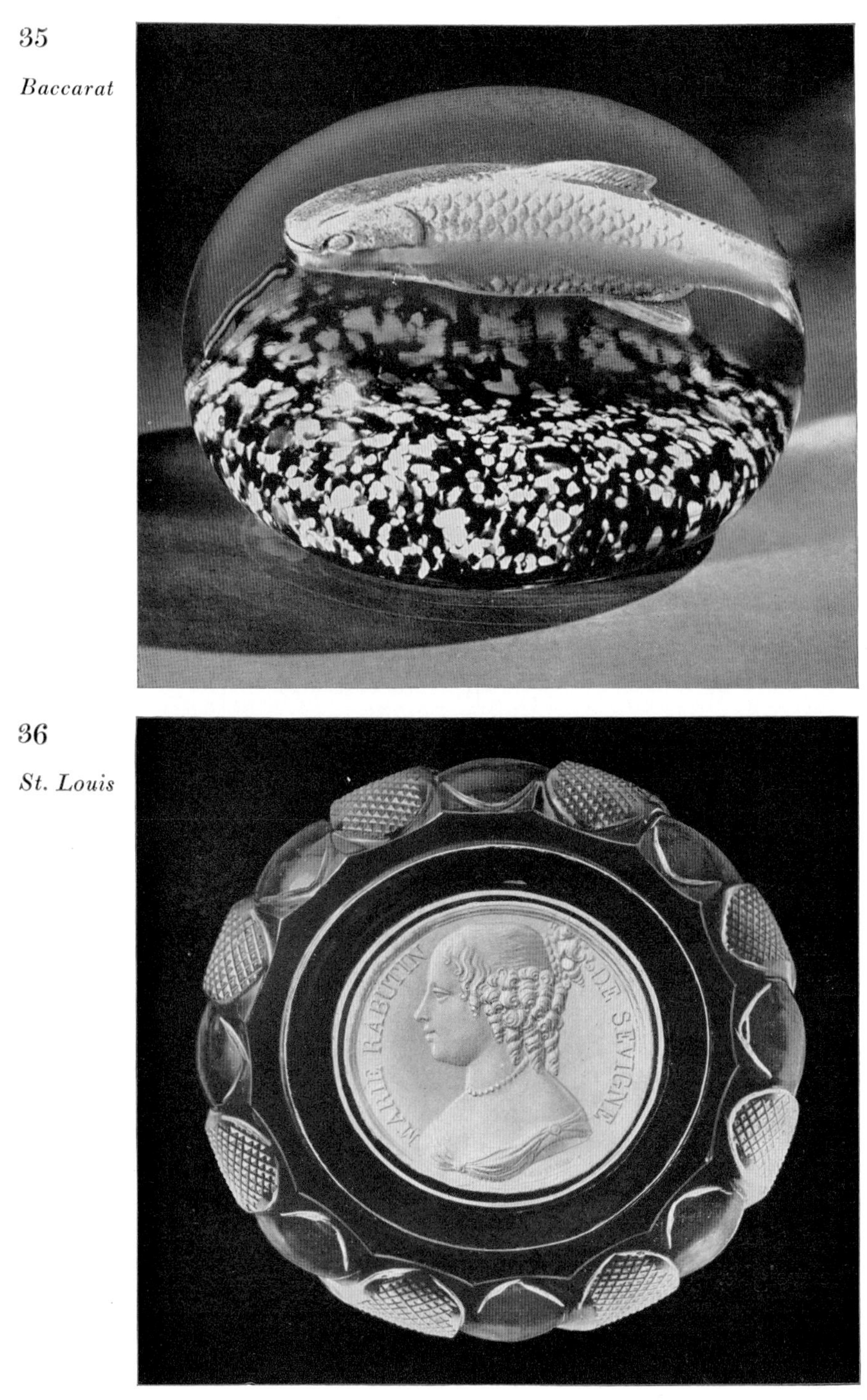

35

Baccarat

36

St. Louis

37

Baccarat

38

Baccarat

ing from that found on French weights (Illustration 33).

Medallions frequently found are those of Count de Chambord, Louis Philippe, Lafayette, Victoria and Albert, in their younger period, and George Washington. The profile of Washington is from a painting by Gilbert Stuart which shows the Roman nose. It is somewhat surprising that we do not find more of the fine profile of Washington by John Trumbull. The foregoing list is by no means complete, for the likenesses of scores of eminent men and women found their way into the cameos.

In the fine sulphide from Baccarat shown in Illustration 35 a silver fish swims, easily, over mottled glass stones near the bottom of the ocean. It may be remarked that the use of the coin shape in another class of weights serves as a point of departure for producing cameos of many other types. (See Illustration 36.)

Many of the sulphides, besides those made at St. Louis, Clichy, and Baccarat, were made in various factories. They were frequently made for merchants and signed with the merchants' monograms. Such a signature indicates a good manufacturer, although it must be recognized that many fine specimens lack any such trade mark.

It was not until 1815 to 1840 that cameos became popular in England. Apsley Pellat (1791-1863), who owned the Falcon glass works in London, took out a patent in 1819 on a proces for making these sulphides which greatly reduced the cost and he called them Crystalio Ceramii. These were made by the same process of encrustation used by the French, employing the composition of fine china clay and super silicate of potash. These were molded under a higher degree of heat than was required for working the glass in which they were encased. It is difficult to identify many of the Pellat sulphides today. Pellat seldom signed any of his work, and he never gave the names of any of the artists who modeled the cameos. Pellat's output was quite limited.

In his book, "Curiosities of Glass Making," Apsley Pellat said, "The ceramics may be painted with metallic colors, which are fixed by exposure to a melting heat. In this way, every description of ornamental glassware has been decorated with every embossed white or colored arms or crest. Miniature landscapes, birds, and flowers are also enameled without losing any of their brilliance; and thus, instead of being painted on the surface of the crystal, they are ornaments embodied in it." Birds, crests, dogs, and flowers are indeed found in the paperweights of Pellat; and, when the patterns are examined, it is found invariably that they are lined at the back with gold.

Pellat found by experiment that a star cutting on the base of the clear glass paperweights was effective in preventing the unpleasant refraction of light which occurred when the base was left plain. When cameo encrustations are applied to such articles as clear glass tumblers, bottles, and boxes, however, the glass on the back of the cameo is always left flat and uncut.

In 1831 Pellat took out a patent for making cameos of clear glass, but these proved to be unattractive and were not successful. It has been said that Pellat thereafter went to France and taught his process in various factories. This he might easily have done, but there appears to be no real authority for this statement. Further information on his later career may perhaps be uncovered in the old records of the workmen in the factories.

The first factory in America known to make cameos was Bakewell, Page & Bakewell of Pittsburgh. This company inserted them in the bottom of their tumblers made around 1830. Apsley Pellat came to this country for a short time in 1840, and it may be that his instructions influenced other factories to undertake their manufacture. Cameos were later used for adorning cup plates, and somewhat later such figures as lambs and dogs were enclosed in crystal marbles to form treasures for children.

The study of ceramics is a field in itself, and one that invites much interesting historical research.

39

Baccarat

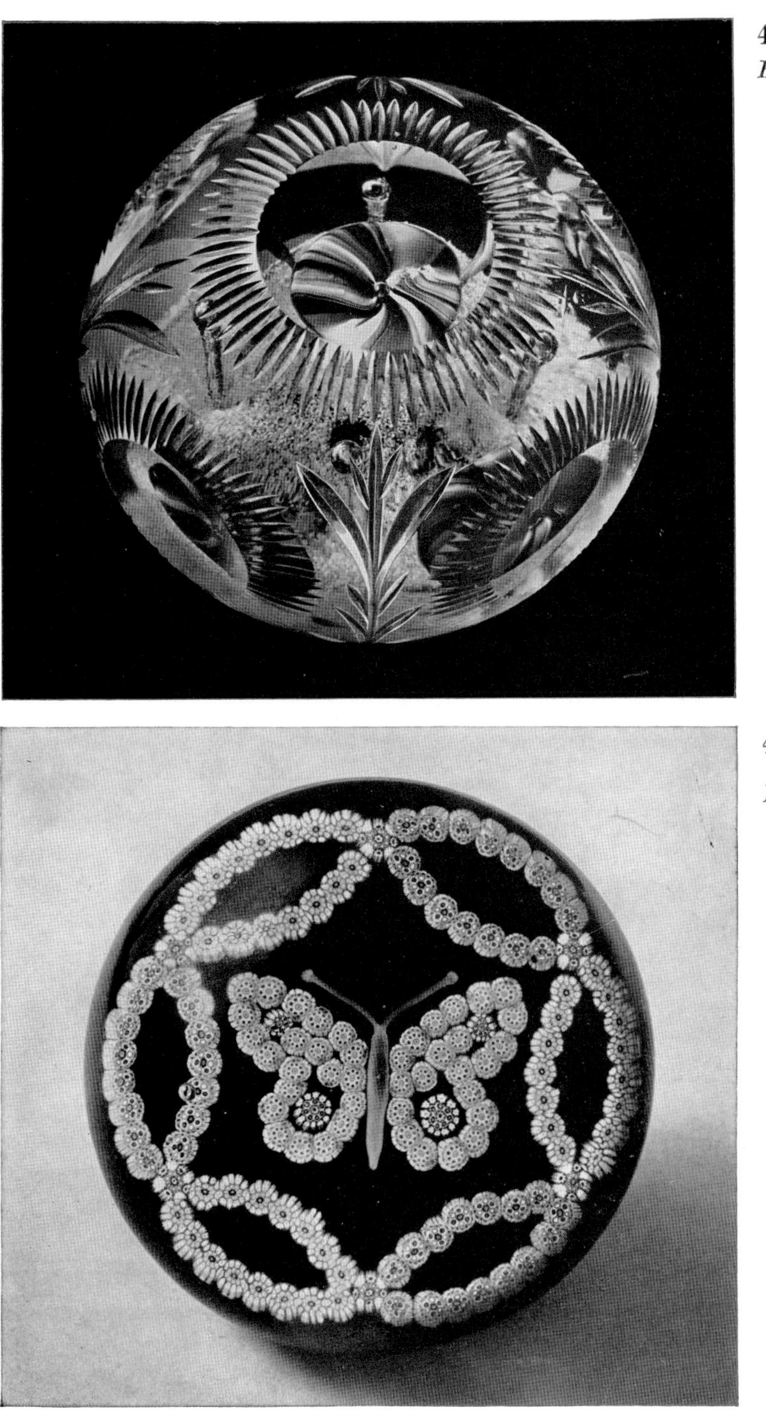

40
Bristol

41
Bristol

IV. ENGLAND

Bristol

THE most important of the English glass centers were London, Bristol, Nailsea, and Stourbridge. The English glass industry received considerable impetus with the introduction of skilled workers from France in the 16th Century. These craftsmen, like the Venetians, were described as gentlemen or esquires, and evidently ranked as persons of honor and consequence. England became an exporter of glass, rather than an importer, during the 18th Century, but it appears that its strong position in the glass industry was due more to the quality of its metal than to any preëminence in decoration or design. We find that around the year 1840 English metal was considered superior to the French. By the time the London Exposition opened in 1851 paperweights had become the rage, and their production was more or less commercialized. Many paperweights were made in England around 1870, but good ones of this period are now rather hard to find. In 1828 Bristol had twelve glass houses, and, next to London, was the most important glass center in England. A familiar feature of Bristol glass is a pear-shaped bubble which was used extensively in old green glass door stops and paperweights. These bubble decorations were made by piercing the hot glass with a sharp pointed instrument to any desired depth or introducing a drop of alcohol. The alcohol, upon coming into contact with the hot glass, produces a bubble. Sometimes the bubbles were arranged to give the effect of a fountain.

An early English weight containing a pink flower has been much copied in modern Czechoslovakian weights. The modern imitation is found on the counters of many gift shops and it is quite hard to distinguish the imitation from the original unless it is known that the antique English weight has a more sandy appearance in the ball and that the pink of the flower is a much lighter shade in the original than in the imitation. (See Illustration 40.)

Glass having an interesting shade of sapphire blue is usually Bristol, but Bristol is by no means always blue. Yellow and opaque white were frequently used. The unusual richness of the characteristic Bristol blue is due to antimony in the sand. Many small birds were made of the Bristol blue glass, and these are interesting despite the fact that they are fashioned somewhat crudely. A butterfly on a sapphire blue background is another good example. (See Illustration 41.)

Illustration 42 shows a blue glass bird on a hollow mottled glass base which contains the colors found in an old Nailsea witch ball.

The opaque and royal blue glass made at Bristol is considered by some to be the finest product from this source. Its brilliant quality often causes it to be mistaken for Venetian glass. It must be recognized that opaque glass has been handed down from ancient days and from many makers. In order to classify paperweights properly, it is therefore necessary to understand the characteristics of the various factories. The Bristol

42

Bristol

43

Bristol

opaque glass is solid white, never yellowish; and, when it is held to the light, it is semi-transparent like certain types of porcelain. It is fairly heavy, and it is entirely free from any bluish cast around the edges. Much of the American opaque is translucent but not transparent, and it has a somewhat cloudy quality. It is also thinner than the English, although both the English and the American are quite fragile. The French opaque, on the other hand, is solid, fairly heavy, and it is not easily chipped or broken. Another identifying feature is its bluish cast.

Isaac Jacobs of the Bristol works made imitations of Venetian glass to great perfection. He was especially successful in glass ornamented with white and colored threads like those we find in paperweights and goblets. Large amounts of faceted glass were also produced, and this helped to spread the fame of Bristol throughout Europe.

A typical Bristol paperweight subject is a deep purple and yellow pansy with green leaves and stem and a star center. While butterfly and fruit subjects were numerous, the small coiled snake on a latticinio background is very rare and much sought after. The weights with the high crown containing a red glass flower-pot out of which grow flowers on a long stem or a cactus design are supposed to be English.

It may be said in general that good English weights are hard to find. Those we have are huge, rather clumsy, and unimpressive—utterly lacking in the delicacy of the French.

Illustration 43 shows an English fake which carries a

date. These, ironically, are now so old that they are worth keeping. It will be observed that these weights have a large date directly in the center. This is in sharp contrast to the French practice of inserting dates in small character and in inconspicuous positions. These weights were probably made for one of the expositions in Paris or London which were held during the height of the paperweight popularity.

Nailsea

Nailsea Glass Works was established in 1788 in Somerset, seven miles from Bristol. It was first operated by John Robert Lucas, a glass maker from Bristol, and it

44

Nailsea

was later taken over by a company which carried on the business until 1873, when it was closed because operations were unprofitable. One advantage of this factory was the excellent grade of coal found under Nailsea heath.

Much of the Nailsea glass is of the Bristol type, following the Venetian in color and style. The factory imported French and Venetian workmen who were experts in latticinio and ribbon effects.

There is a tradition that these early Nailsea workers were a bad and immoral lot, and it is recorded that in 1792 two hundred of them, of all ages and both sexes, lived in a row of nineteen houses. It is not surprising to learn that these people were superstitious and that they originated the so-called "witch balls." These witch balls were hung in windows or from rafters as charms to ward off the evil eye. The witch ball had a hole in its bottom, and a knot was tied in a string and placed inside the opening, which was then closed by a cork. Similar balls without the opening sometimes served as covers for sugar bowls and cream pitchers. Small hollow glass balls were used by fishermen in America for bobbers, and larger ones served as floats for nets. Blue glass balls, sometimes eight inches in diameter, were also made at Nailsea, and it was claimed that these had a therapeutic value. This was the simplest form of glass blowing. These balls were often made from a mixture of colors as part of the training of apprentices.

Superstition surrounded another object made by the Nailsea workers—namely, a cane which was from three to fifteen feet long. Canes of this kind were kept in the houses of the workers, and they were cleaned each morning on the theory that in this way all disease would be driven away. If a cane was broken, misfortune was sure to follow.

The high-crowned green glass paperweights with the filmy or silver flower pots out of which grows a flower of the same composition are from Nailsea; likewise the weight containing the small bubble-formed pattern. These were made in the latter part of the 19th Century. All the earlier weights were of a light green shade. (See Illustration 44.)

It is often difficult to distinguish between Bristol and Nailsea green glass. It may be claimed, however, that the brighter pieces are Bristol and the softer colors are Nailsea—while the very softest of all the greens are Castleford.

The Nailsea output was varied and unusual. It included scent bottles; double headed flasks, varying in height from 3½ to 10½ inches, with pink, blue, or milky white ribbon loops; rolling pins; bells; walking sticks; pipes; and sweetmeat glasses. The coach horn of white glass, 40 inches long, was used to hand up drinks to the drivers of the old stage coaches. Despite the belief of most people that glass tea and coffee urns are modern innovations, glass tea kettles with acorn knobs were made many years ago at Nailsea.

The Nailsea factory never produced cut glass—the only cutting known was in their occasional production of small squares of window glass.

Many of the well-made forgeries of Bristol and Nail-

PLATE XIII. *Baccarat*

PLATE XIV. *Belgian*

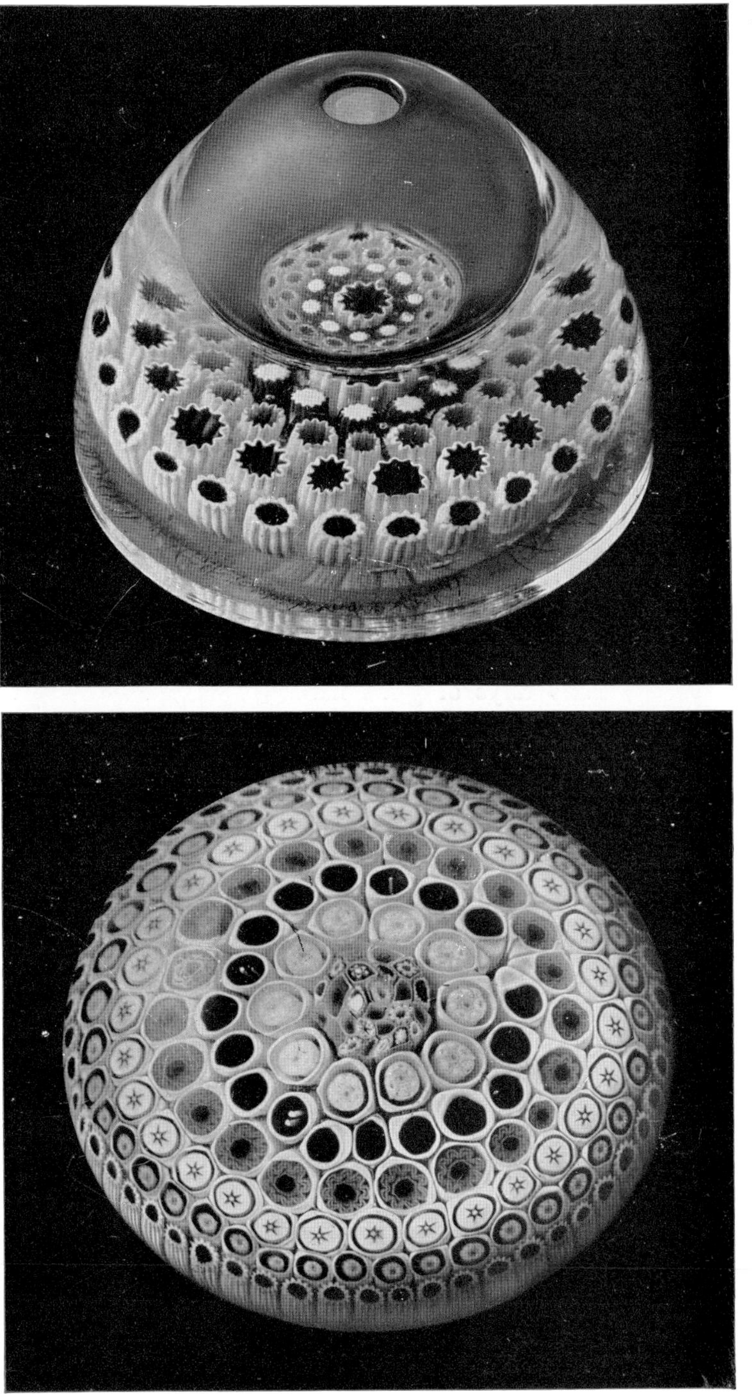

45

Stourbridge

46

Stourbridge

sea glass come from Birmingham where they are aged with the aid of acids.

Stourbridge

The manufacture of glass at Stourbridge in Worcestershire was established by emigrants from Hungary in 1556. The place where they erected their factory is still known as Hungary Hill.

In later years the Stourbridge factory carried on the manufacture of glass at Cork and Waterford, in Ireland.

The clay in the home district is still unsurpassed for use in the making of fire pots in the slow Stourbridge process which consumes from four to six months in baking and drying.

In the early days of glass making in America, great quantities of this clay were shipped, coming over as ballast on the small ships. This was made into fire pots here until clay was discovered in 1815 in Delaware, whereupon the importation of the English product fell off.

Ink bottles were the specialty at Stourbridge. Two pieces from this factory, an ink bottle and a paperweight, are shown in Illustrations 45 and 46. The Stourbridge colors are usually soft and pleasing, resembling those of St. Louis. Stourbridge also uses the deep-well set-ups similar to those used in the St. Louis factory but the texture is coarser, as the ink well in the illustration shows. The resemblances referred to are not accidental, but are accounted for by the fact that the Stourbridge industry brought many of its best workmen from the

St. Louis factory. Stourbridge weights rank among the finest that have come from England.

London

A high crown is a distinguishing characteristic of many of the English paperweights. This is not true, however, of those made at White Friars, which is the trade name for the James Powell Glass Works, founded in 1680 and located outside of London. Glass is made in this factory in the same manner as it was made a century ago. The sand used is almost pure silica, and all of it comes from Fontainebleau. Until 1845 only flint glass was made at White Friars.

The White Friars people describe their set-ups as Victorian flower clusters, and these have been used in ink bottles as well as in paperweights (Illustrations 47 and 48). Only one date is known in the White Friars' product, namely, in 1848; and this is easy to distinguish and remember because of the peculiar figures used in its formation. White Friars has made great advances in the quality of glass and in the beauty of its colors, and their work in stained glass is most important.

A splendid example of their craftsmanship is found in the huge Gothic stained glass windows in St. Thomas' Church in New York City.

The English glass industry has been subject to various vicissitudes during its long history. The glass excise act of 1745, for example, taxed glass by weight, with the result that the factories reduced the proportion of lead and thereby impaired the quality of much of their production. The English are entitled to second place in

47

White Friars

48

White Friars

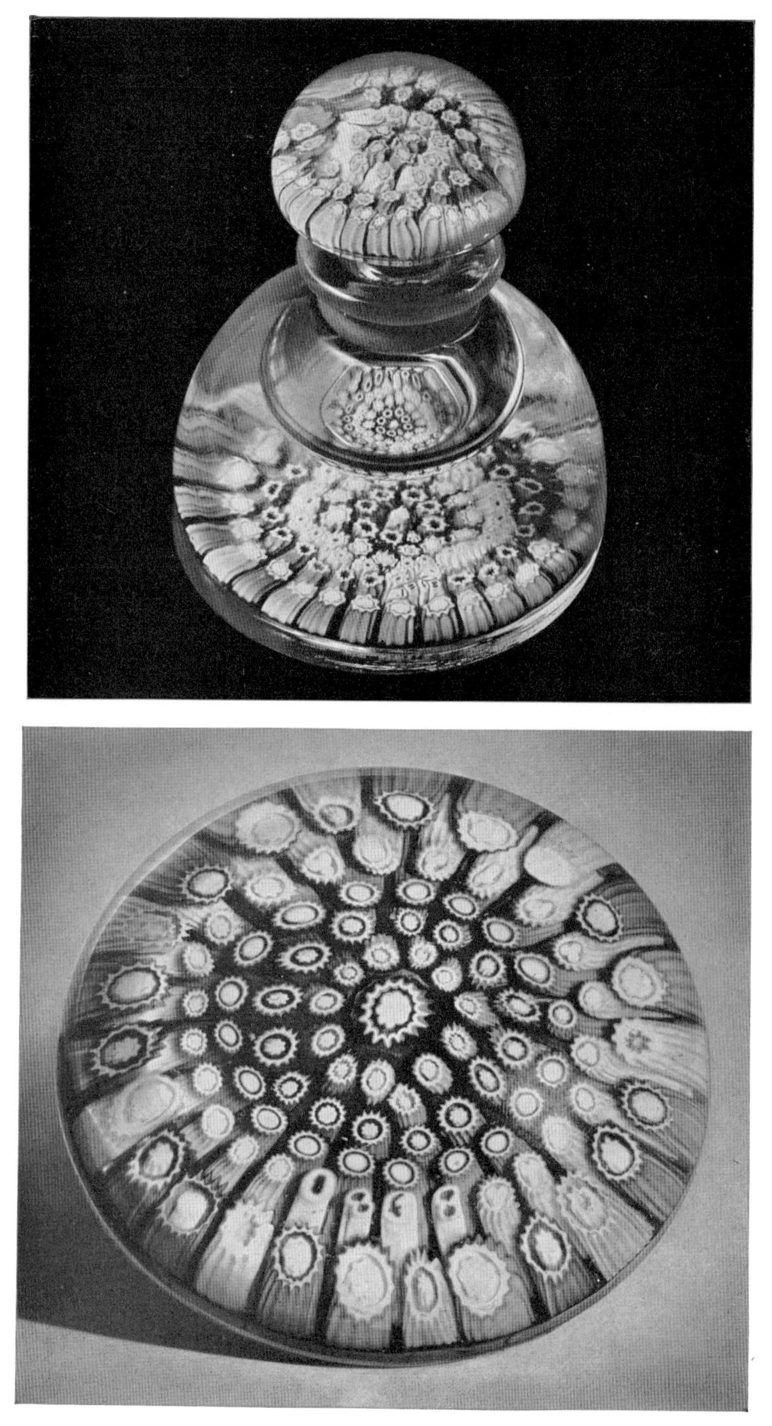

the production of fine clear glass—there is no question that the French have led all other nations. The Americans rank next to the British, while the Irish come last. No flux was used in the glass made in Irish factories, and for this reason the product bore close resemblance to rock crystal. The making of glass paperweights passed out in England with the era of Victorian bric-a-brac, and interest in the art was not again revived until about 1920.

The glass which has come from the various English factories is so hard to classify clearly and definitely that we may some day give up the struggle to bring order out of chaos and simply group the products of all British factories together under the general head of English glass.

V. MINOR EUROPEAN SOURCES

Venetian

ALTHOUGH the Venetians occupied an important position in the history of glass making, their work does not, in the opinion of the writer, entitle them to a first rank position among makers of fine old paperweights. Their colors are rather dull and their workmanship inferior. Venetian weights suffer by comparison with the better French product. The glass used, in the first place, has a lime base, is light in weight and is easily broken. Instead of a set-up in the center, Venetian weights usually have a bubble or a circular opening. The Venetian weight shown in Illustration 49 is of blown glass, hollow, with an alternating gold twist and opaque blue stripe.

The Venetians deserve credit for being the first to invent engraving upon glass, a process which soon spread throughout Europe. They etched their first engraved specimen with a diamond, but they later invented a wheel of copper and lead which worked much faster and better. Much colored enamel glass was used by the Venetians and the flint glass is extremely elastic and may be spun so thin as to bend double without breaking.

Apsley Pellatt gives an interesting description of one method used by the Venetians in making their millefiori weight. They began by taking a double transparent cone, placing the cone between two surfaces. Heat was then applied and the blow pipe was used to draw the air out of the double case. Upon being rewarmed, this structure was formed into a homogeneous mass around which the outer structure of the paperweight could be built. This process was widely different from any employed in other factories which produced paperweights. The filigree twist was used quite extensively, and another specialty was Mosaic glass. The extent to which the Venetians were interested in glass of this time is indicated by the fact that there were 300 glass houses at Murano at the beginning of the 17th Century, although at the beginning of the present century only one mosaic factory remained and this was closed in 1925. Later the owner, a man named Trade, was persuaded to open it for the purpose of renewing the mosaics in St. Mark's, and this

49

Venetian

brought about the greatest revival in the glass industry of the present day. An example of the smetz glass produced by this factory is found in a wigstand in the Metropolitan Museum. This was made by rolling lumps of colored glass one into another to imitate agate and other stones. Another specimen consists of fine lace work called Vitro ditrina, which contains fine patterns of intersecting lines of white enamel and transparent glass evenly divided into diamond shaped sections, with an air bubble of uniform size in the center of each.

Belgian

The Val Saint Lambert factory was established in a Cistercian Abbey near Seraing in Belgium. It was founded by John Cockerill (1790–1840), an Englishman, and eventually became one of the largest enterprises of its kind in Europe. At one time it employed as many as 5,000 workmen. The glass produced was of fine quality, and rivaled that of England and France. Another Val Saint Lambert factory was founded in 1825 by two Frenchmen named Lelievere and Kemlin. This factory reached its greatest development later under the management of Jules Deprez. It is still running today, and is as famous in Belgium as St. Louis and Baccarat in France.

Val Saint Lambert produced paperweights in a great variety of designs and forms, all of which were made on a large scale. Val Saint Lambert used a remarkably thin overlay—which, however, is distinctly not flash. A design was cut through this overlay, revealing the center pattern. Val Saint Lambert's patterns, unfortunately, are rather unattractive.

It may be said parenthetically at this point that flash can be recognized in the following manner. If you look through a weight along the edges where it has been cut or etched, and if you find along these edges a chip or scratch that looks white, you may be reasonably sure that the specimen is treated with flash and not genuine overlay. Flash is blown on or applied with a brush, never dipped as in the genuine old process. The Val Saint Lambert weight shown in Plate XIV is a blue cut overlay with a pink opaque center. Over the center are four twisted loops of white opaque glass interspersed with bubbles. Another similar twist lies on the outside rim of the center pattern. This weight, with its extremely high crown, is as interesting as it is unusual.

German

Germany produced relatively few weights, and the metals used in German weights were heated over coal fires, with the result that they lacked the clearness and luster which has been noted in the fine product of St. Louis, Baccarat and Clichy. Bright colors were used invariably in German weights, and the decorative composition tended to be heavy, rather than delicate and graceful.

Perhaps the commonest of the German weights is the type employing a calla lily which has a bubble for a stamen. The lily was formed from many small blotches of colored glass. The floral pattern of the weight was placed around a high center-motif which often had the same color composition as the flower.

There are few German weights found in America today, and it is possible that even these were made in this country by German workmen, for the early Massachusetts factories employed many Germans about the year 1780. One American factory which was entirely owned and governed by Germans in Colonial days was located at Fredericktown in Maryland.

The fondness of German workmen for using enamel makes their work somewhat reminiscent of the Venetian, but any examination and comparison of the result reveals the Venetian enamel as having a distinctly finer quality.

Bohemian

It was in Bohemia that the art of etching on glass with fluoric acid was discovered in 1670. The substance of most Bohemian glass is potash. This produces an extraordinarily hard glass which lends itself readily to deep intaglio engraving. This process of etching on glass, by the way, was first used in America at the Cambridge factory soon after the Revolutionary War.

Bohemian glass was in great demand during the Mid-Victorian period. A piece of Bohemian engraved ruby glass was an almost inevitable decoration on every table or mantel of that time. Paperweights of the millefiori type were produced in Bohemia from 1840 to 1850. A few of these have survived with others of the cameo type (Illustration 33).

From an old print, courtesy of Henry Ford Museum

The Sandwich Glass Works about 1829

VI. AMERICA

Early Beginnings

THE history of glass making in America follows the record of settlement in Virginia, Pennsylvania, New Jersey, New York, and New England, and the migrations westward to the Ohio Valley. Associated with the early days of the glass industry were the names of Wistar and Stiegel, but these came long before the days of Sandwich . . . before the glass makers of young America had tried their hand at making paperweights. The story of the early adventurers into the field of glass manufacture is still quite obscure and confused. Much remains to be done by research workers and historians before the haze is cleared away from this department of our industrial history. For our present purposes it will be sufficient to note that the glass industry gained a foothold in this country as a result of the great need of the early settlers for window glass. In colonial times window glass was used as ballast in vessels sailing from Europe to America. The breakage was so great, however, that the price was prohibitive, and the colonists began to take thought whether they could not somehow supply their own necessities.

The first factory in America was a glass furnace established at Jamestown, Virginia, in 1607. A site was chosen in the woods, in order that there might be abundant fuel for smelting purposes, as well as logs to use in building the factory and homes for the workers. Teams of oxen brought in the sand and clay over a rough road, and took out the finished product on the return journey. When it became possible to deliver the finished glass by water, the breakage became considerably less. Despite all the efforts that were made to reduce costs, however, the window glass produced by this factory was too expensive for most settlers, and found only a limited market. Eventually, therefore, the factory changed from window glass to the making of bottles and beads for trading with the Indians for land, food and fur. Some of these little early American beads, green and white in color and similar in size to gooseberries, have been found in excavations. Specimens are understood to be in museums at Philadelphia and Toledo. The glass works was destroyed at the time of the great Indian Massacre at Jamestown in 1622, and some of the surviving workmen migrated later as far as Pennsylvania and Massachusetts.

During the period of the American Revolution, many new factories were established in Massachusetts, New York, Eastern Pennsylvania, New Jersey, and Maryland. Coal was first used in this country for the smelting of glass at Pittsburgh in 1797. Later, with the discovery of coal and oil in Western Pennsylvania, Virginia, Ohio, and Indiana, the American glass industry began to move westward. Eventually, the great valleys of the Ohio and Mississippi became leading centers of glass manufacture in the United States.

Sandwich

Much of the fame achieved by the glass industry in Massachusetts centers about one man, Deeming Jarves (1791–1869). Jarves was a man of unusual vision, and his sound business methods, his inventiveness, and his artistic ability entitle him to a preëminent position among the glassmakers of his day. With four associates, he organized the New England Glass Company at East Cambridge, Massachusetts, in 1817. Here he received the training which was destined to lead to many brilliant accomplishments. In 1825 he decided to have a glass factory of his own and proceeded to erect it at Sandwich, on Cape Cod. This location was not chosen on account of the sand, for this was of poor quality, but for the abundance of wood which could be used for smelting purposes. Glass furnaces, as has already been suggested, require careful and uniform feeding by men called shearers or tenders in order to produce the finest quality of glass. Sandwich offered another advantage in that the glass products could be sent to Boston by water or overland, and later over a small railway which was the first rail transportation line in America.

In 1837 Jarves started another glass factory for his son, George, at South Boston, Massachusetts, and called this the Mount Washington Glass Company. He eventually withdrew from this company after a quarrel with some of his directors, and in 1858 he founded the Cape Cod Glass Works. This plant he operated until his death in 1869.

The history of the Sandwich glass factory finally came to an end as a result of a disagreement with its workers. It is rather surprising, as a matter of fact, that conflicts with labor did not arise more frequently than they did in the glass industry. Few people who are not acquainted with the conditions under which glass must be made have any realization of the tremendous heat to which the glass blower was subjected in the early days of the industry—heat so great that it was reputed to bring about a material reduction of the life span of the worker. A bulletin published by the Boston and Sandwich Company in 1854 made the claim that no workman had died or was seriously ill as a result of his employment during the preceding twenty years. This statement, assuming it to be true, reflected an important improvement in working conditions, but it is likely that the improvement was only relative. In December 1887 the Glass Association presented an agreement to the employees of the various factories with the request that they subscribe to its terms. This the Sandwich workmen refused to do, and a strike followed. Having operated the company at a loss for some time previously, the manage-

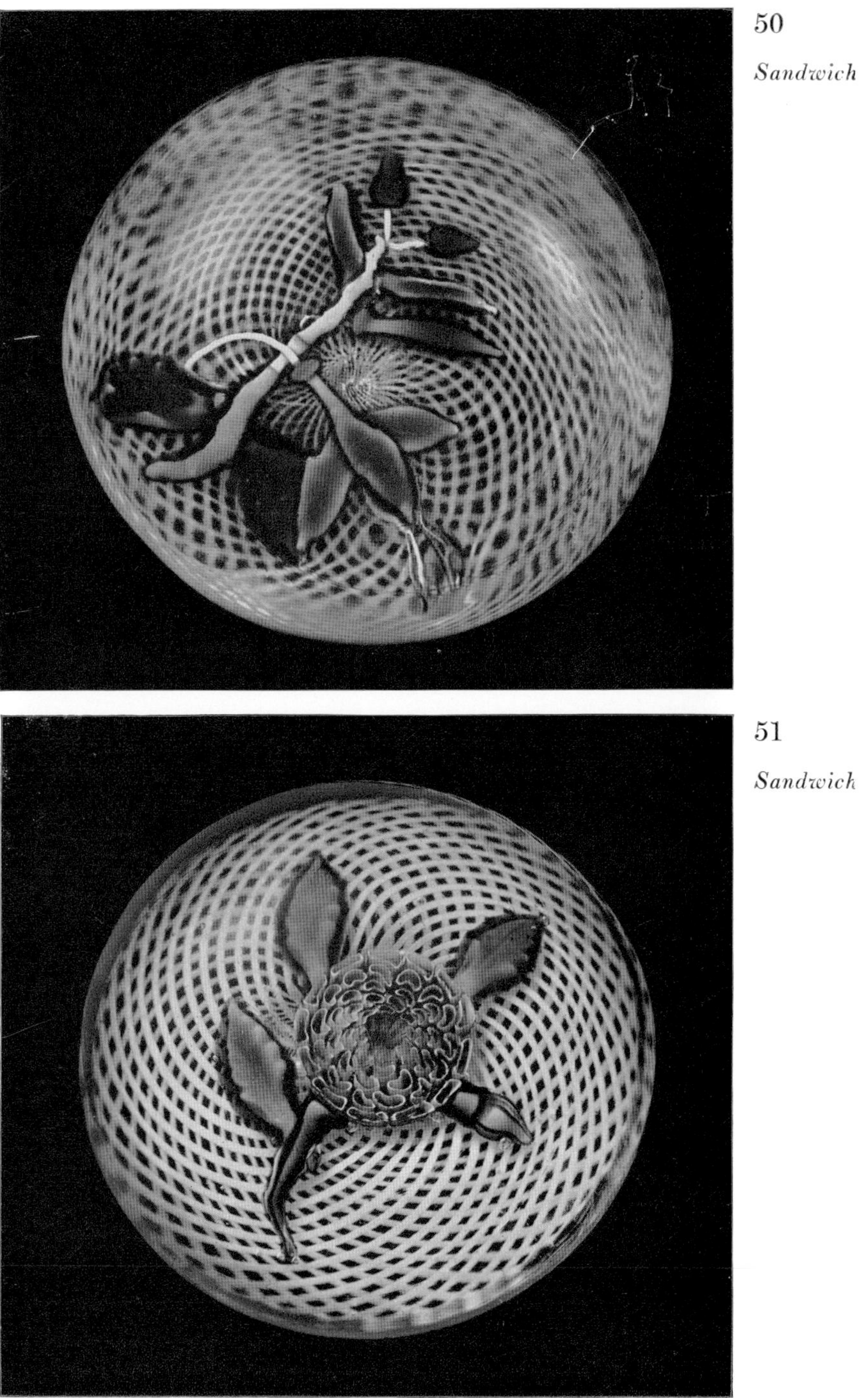

50

Sandwich

51

Sandwich

ment informed the men that if the furnaces were ever allowed to go out, they would never be re-lighted. The men refused to take this threat seriously, but the management proved to be as good as its word—the plant was closed in 1888, and was never again reopened.

During the 62 years of its existence, the Sandwich factory made glass for many purposes. Paperweights were made by an Austrian workman with an unpronounceable name, who, for convenience, called himself Timothy Collins; and by a Frenchman named Nicholas Lutz, who was one of the gaffers or foremen of the company. The paperweights that came from the hands of these men were especially fine. Evidence that it must have taken the factory a long time to produce paperweights of excellent quality is found in the fact that great numbers of imperfect weights have been taken from an old well on the premises.

The metal used in the Sandwich glass was of superb quality and great brilliancy. It is probable that no factory of today manufactures better glass. An interesting feature of some of the Sandwich weights were the flecks of gold incorporated in them.

The Sandwich factory was the first to adopt and perfect the process of producing fine glass in a mold under pressure, rather than by the traditional method of blowing. The molding process was invented by a workman named Enoch Robinson. This process was later borrowed and used by Baccarat.

In 1849 Deeming Jarves gave to the chemists of the Boston and Sandwich Company a set of color formulas published by Apsley Pellatt. This they were instructed

PLATE XV. *Baccarat*

PLATE XVI. *Sandwich*

to follow. The colors in Sandwich glass resemble those of the Baccarat factory, from which many of the Sandwich workmen were drawn. Certainly, no other factory excelled Sandwich in the perfection and range of its colors. A book of formulas for colored glass which was prepared in 1868 by James D. Lloyd for the use of Sandwich workmen, is now owned by Henry Ford. It shows no less than thirty shades of blue, and the range of other colors included is correspondingly wide.

Among the Sandwich paperweights, the millefiori and candy type are quite common. The flower and fruit subjects have a distinction which is admirably illustrated by the fuchsia, with its pink stem—quite comparable with the same subject in Baccarat which often has a yellow stem. (Illustration 50.) The pink poinsettia was the favorite Sandwich flower and the example in Illustration 2 shows the drops of dew on the petals. The dahlia has the appearance of being made at the Baccarat factory, but from the composition of the glass we know it is Sandwich. (See Illustration 51.) This is also found sometimes in purple or blue, with a bud and leaves on either a clear, mottled or latticinio background. The pansy is treated similarly in Sandwich weights, and is often hard to distinguish from the same subject in Bristol. This is perhaps explained by the fact that many of the workmen came from the Bristol factory.

Among the fruit weights the strawberry takes first place, although not many of these were produced. Illustration 52 shows a weight containing five strawberries, with blossoms and leaves, which is so beautifully done that the berries look good enough to eat. This is

52

Sandwich

53

Sandwich

54

Clichy

55

Baccarat

being copied today in a larger weight with lighter green leaves. Another fruit weight is shown in Illustration 53.

Among the door knobs shown in Illustrations 54, 55 and 56 we see three examples: one is a Clichy; one a Baccarat with cameos of Lafayette in one knob and Franklin in the other; and the third is an elaborately cut, mercury-filled type made at Sandwich. Deeming Jarves took out two patents on door knobs in 1840, and many of those made in his factory resemble copies of paperweights.

In their lamp room at Sandwich small glass buttons were made containing small roses and green leaves and resembling miniature paperweights. These can easily be distinguished from similar buttons made at the factory

57

Sandwich, date reversed

58

Sandwich

in Muncie, Indiana, because the latter had blue leaves. Sandwich paperweights are occasionally found which bear the date 1852. A few were made with the last two figures transposed on the center flower so that the date reads 1825, but we know that this is an error because they were not being made at that date. One of these is shown in Illustration 57.

Sandwich tried to imitate the lacy bead effect achieved by the St. Louis factory in plates and vases, but their results were crude in comparison. They also tried to copy the St. Louis crown weight, but again the results were inferior, and it is not hard to distinguish between the two products.

Sandwich also took up the Potichomania craze, which was fostered by Godey's Lady's Book in 1855. This consisted of applying pictures or decalcomania transfers to the interior of bottle-green blown glass balls and paperweights, a proceeding requiring some degree of skill. Before placing the picture on the glass, a thin coating of gum arabic was applied. Then, when the picture had been placed in position, a coat of varnish was laid over all and the ball was lined with paint (Illustration 58). Witch balls, made in somewhat the same fashion, were usually left hollow. These were covered with a thin plaster-like substance, and, when finished, had a small opening in the base.

The Sandwich Company used no marks whatsoever to identify their products. It is entirely possible that much of the glass which has been attributed to them actually came from other glass works in New England, Ohio, or Pittsburgh—or perhaps even from England.

They seldom advertised, and many of their wares were distributed by peddlers going about the country. Such peddlers usually carried one or two weights in their wagons with other articles.

The collecting of fine paperweights has gone on ever since the days in which they were produced. It is understood that a collector in Boston at one time owned more than 100 millefiori weights. On account of the large amount of hand work required, a good millefiori weight was never cheap. Its cost, even from the beginning, ranged from $5.00 upward. Workmen received $14.00 to $17.00 a week in wages, and a good deal of time was required to produce a weight of fine quality.

It has been estimated that products worth $30,000,-000.00 were sold by the Sandwich factory during the long period of its operation—no mean total considering the industrial and commercial development of the era in which this enterprise carried on its operations.

New England Glass Works

The first American furnace for making lead glass is supposed to have been built by Deeming Jarves at the New England Glass Works, East Cambridge, Massachusetts, in 1818. This company made many molded and candy type fruit weights like those made at Sandwich, but all its blown fruit weights were made at Cambridge. The finest of the paperweights which came from the New England factory were made by François Pierre, who came from Baccarat; and by another workman named John Hopkins, whose output was large up to the year 1874.

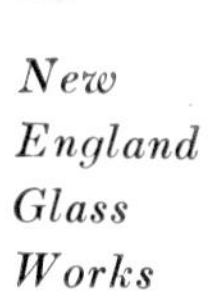
59

New England Glass Works

60

New England Glass Works

The New England Works had a great variety of molds for flowers, animals, letters, figures, and the filigree rods and stars, all of which were combined to form the endlessly varied patterns in the weights.

From the New England factory came millefiori paperweights as well as apples, pears, and ceramic subjects; and at least one millefiori weight bearing the date 1854. The blown apple and pear weights were fashioned by blowing the glass from a tube in such a way that the fruit came out red on one side and yellow or green on the other. In shaping the glass as it came from the tube it was expanded to the size desired, drawn in at the end and finished with small pieces of dark glass to form such

61

New England Glass Works

objects as blossom and stem. The expansion caused by the fusing of the two colors in the tube contributed to an interesting result. After blowing, the fruit section was fused to a round crystal mold which formed the base. Sometimes Mr. Pierre added leaves to his apples and pears, and these helped to make his pieces distinctive. (See Illustrations 59 and 60.)

New England began making ceramics about the time of the London Exposition, but their cameos failed to achieve the fine silvery appearance of those made by the French. The effect is decidedly duller. Most widely known of the ceramics produced at this factory was the silhouette of Victoria and Albert (Illustration 61), although their weights using the head of Washington and Lincoln rank among their very best. It should perhaps be noted that the Gillerland Company also produced a paperweight using the head of Queen Victoria in profile, similar to that in the New England weight just mentioned. Some excellent ceramics were also made by Washington Beck during the seventies at the Curling and Pierce factory in Pittsburgh. These medallions, however, never equalled the fine workmanship of those made in France and England. They were, in fact, rather crude in comparison. These are not often encountered.

Green glass turtles are still found which were popular at the time of the Civil War. Turtles of one kind were produced in a factory at Lancaster, New York, but the weight from this source has a much rounder shape than those made at Sandwich or Cambridge. In the later days of the Cambridge factory, from 1860 to 1875, production there was treated as much more of a commercial process and its weights were turned out by the hundreds.

It was in the Cambridge factory, about 1848, that a process was discovered for making ruby glass. This was done by melting a gold piece into the mixture. Prior to that time, all the ruby glass used in this country was imported from England.

Trade secrets were guarded carefully in this factory as in every other. The book of formulas used by William Leighton, their first gaffer or superintendent, passed—presumably through the hands of the six sons who followed the vocation of glass making after his death—into the possession of his grandson, Thomas Leighton, where it still remains.

In 1878 the Cambridge Works were leased by W. L. Libbey, whose son moved the factory to Toledo, Ohio, nine years later. This location was chosen because natural gas had been discovered in the Toledo area. This meant an abundant supply of cheap fuel which is excellent for the purposes of the glass industry.

Since Deeming Jarves was closely connected with the factories both at Cambridge and Sandwich, it is not surprising that the paperweights coming from both places should bear a marked resemblance. The constant interchange of workmen between the two factories is no doubt a further factor accounting for the similarity.

The migrations of workmen between different factories, even between factories in different countries, may account for similarities that can hardly be explained in any other way. At the same time it must be remembered that men, while they carry their abilities from one factory to another, could not take with them the silica and other material which they had used. The quality of the glass in a paperweight is therefore a cardinal point in determining the country from which it came. The French glass for example is characteristically clear and sharp; English glass has a heavy, cloudy quality; the American product has more of the melted sugar appearance, with many swirl effects that are apparent if the casing is examined at an angle. These swirl effects are especially pronounced in Sandwich weights. Visible swirls, by the way, are not particularly significant. Those which are invisible to the eye and can be seen only through the polariscope are an entirely different matter. These indi-

62

Mount Washington

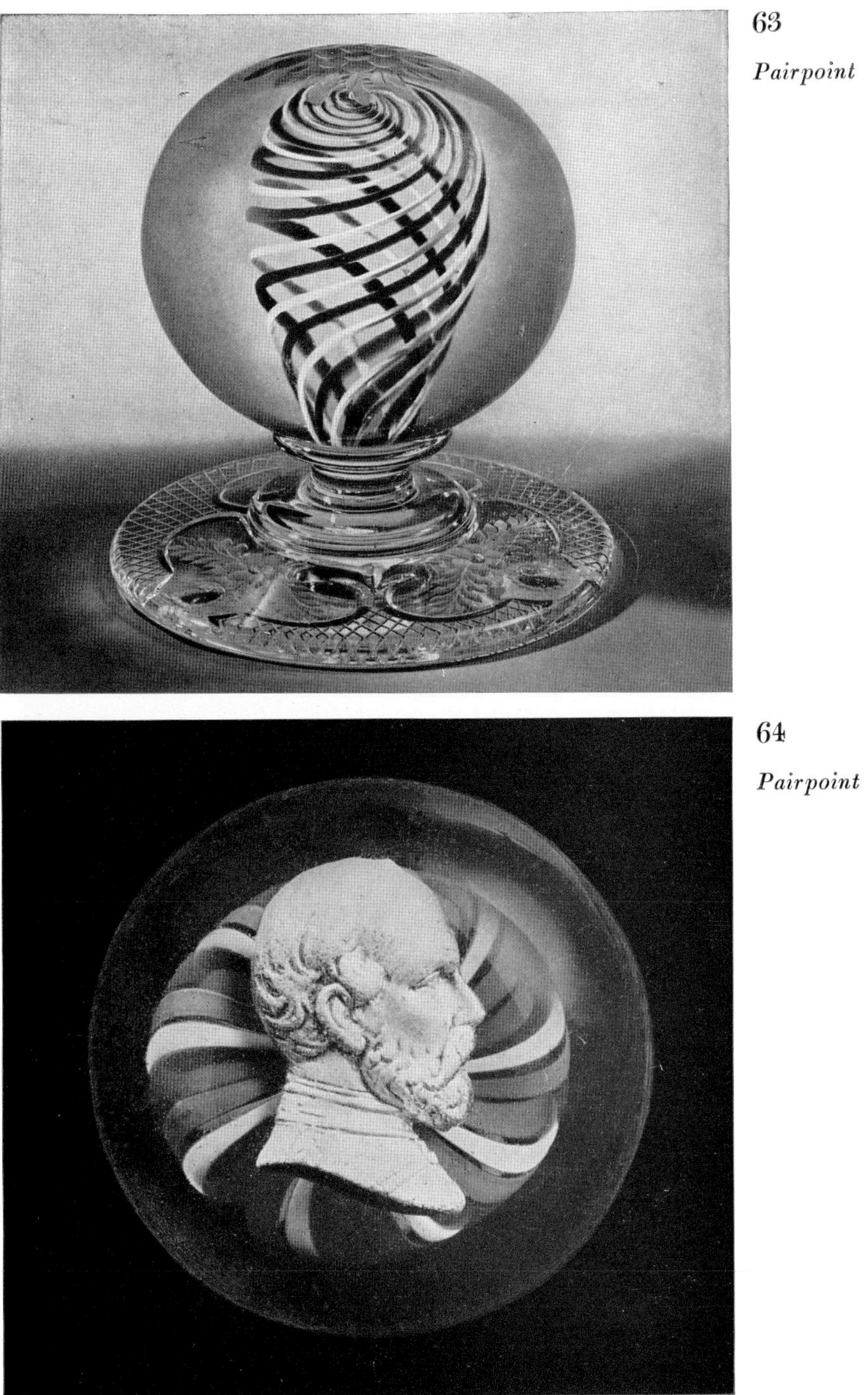

63

Pairpoint

64

Pairpoint

cate the tiny cracks which are caused by improper annealing, and they are serious because they often lead to cracking that occurs without apparent reason.

Mount Washington

One of the very finest of all American paperweights came from the Mount Washington Factory at South Boston, Massachusetts. This factory, it will be remembered, was established in 1837 by Deeming Jarves for his son, George. The name was dropped when this factory was absorbed by the New England Glass Company at the time when ownership passed to W. L. Libbey.

The weight in question shown in Illustration 62, is a large specimen of which the most striking feature is a beautifully frilled rose in shades of salmon pink. This rose is held in a woman's hand which is ornamented with a gold ring. Forming something of a bouquet with the rose are two buds, many leaves, and certain items of small fruit. Two butterflies hover over the rose, one at each side. The center of the rose is flecked with gold and similar gold fragments are scattered over the petals. The gold flecks are similar to those found in many Sandwich weights.

This Mount Washington rose weight illustrates the use of the best American metal. The finest glass sand available in America today is pumped from the bottom of Oneida Lake in New York State—a supply which may be endless. The second finest quality comes from West Virginia, and the third from the Berkshires near Pittsfield, where the Sandwich factory found its sand. Silica sand of good quality comes also from Ottawa, Illinois,

65

Somerville

66

Tiffany

which is the source of supply for many middle-western factories.

Pairpoint

The Pairpoint Company was established at New Bedford, Massachusetts, in 1865.

Pairpoint is notable for its use of the "gray" type of cutting, made by smoothing the cuts in the surface of the weight with a stone and omitting to polish these cuts to a transparent state. In the beginning Pairpoint used the old pinwheel, various stars, and the fan design, but more natural lines were adopted later to harmonize with their patterns.

Cobalt blue and ruby were favorite Pairpoint colors, and the red appears in the decorative spiral twist in the paperweight shown, as well as the gray cut in the flower on both top and base (Illustration 63). A Pairpoint weight showing the head of General Robert E. Lee against a spiral background treatment in red, white, and blue is one of the most attractive of all the American ceramics (Illustration 64). This factory never undertook enameling.

The Pairpoint factory was taken over in 1880 by W. L. Libbey, who built a large addition and changed the name to Mount Washington Glass Works. In applying the same name to two different factories, Libbey contributed at least moderately to the problem of determining sources.

Somerville

The "Three Little Pigs" of nursery story fame were represented in glass by Philip Banano at Somerville,

PLATE XVII. *Unknown*

PLATE XVIII. *Millville*

Massachusetts, long before their exploits were celebrated in the motion picture by Walt Disney. They and their offspring have come down to us through many reproductions in ceramics, wood, and glass. The Union Glass Works, where Banano was employed, was taken over by the South Ferry Glass Company of Brooklyn in 1864 and was operated under the management of that company until 1868. The factory was then moved to Corning, New York, and in 1875 was reorganized as the Corning Glass Works, which is today one of the largest and finest in the world. (See Illustration 65.)

The name and reputation of the Corning Glass Works has done much to bring public realization that glass is now one of the most widely used and essential materials in our industrial civilization. Among the astonishing modern achievements of Corning is a glass which is as resistant to high temperature and as transparent to certain rays as quartz. This product is made from 96% pure silica. In marveling over the modern achievements of a company like Corning, it is at the same time a satisfaction to reflect that a product made by this company, the beautiful, engraved Steuben glass, is highly prized today in the Museums of both America and Europe.

While we express our admiration at the achievements of great modern manufacturers like Corning we feel regret that the conditions of industrial operation have so far changed that certain of the beautiful and artistic objects formerly made of glass are no longer produced. They are no longer made, simply because they do not pay.

We are reminded that the elder Louis Tiffany undertook some experiments in making glass paperweights about the year 1880. He encountered so many difficulties in technique and found his costs rising to such prohibitive levels that he soon discontinued his efforts in this direction. One of Tiffany's experimental products is shown in Illustration 66. This is a large door stop which represents sea urchins at the bottom of the ocean, with dark wavy lines rising about them, perhaps intended to suggest waves.

Millville, New Jersey

One of the most famous and most desirable of all the American antique paperweights is the Jersey rose, which was the product of the Whitall, Tatum Company at Millville, New Jersey. This company established its factory at Millville in 1849 on the site of an old factory that had passed out of existence.

At Millville, Ralph Barber, Michael Kane, Marcus Kuntz, John Rhulander, and Emil Stanger all made paperweights, but it was really Ralph Barber whose workmanship brought this subject to the point of highest beauty and distinction. It is said that Barber learned the art of making paperweights from a workman in the Sandwich factory, who made a crude rose weight without leaves and without a foot. It took Barber six years to bring the weight to its final perfection. Innumerable obstacles were encountered before the Jersey rose became a success at the hands of Barber. His brother George who worked at the Libbey Glass Works in Ohio sent him ruby glass from there; but this, like many other samples obtained elsewhere, had expansion characteristics which were not suited to the body, and there was endless difficulty with cracking. The crack which caused the trouble appeared on the inside of the weight around the rose; it never extended to the surface. A glass was finally found at the E. P. Gleason factory in Brooklyn, New York, which had a lime base and the same coefficiency of expansion as the Millville crystal, and with this discovery the Jersey rose finally became a success.

In an old account book of the Gleason Company is recorded a shipment of 150 pounds of ruby glass, 15 pounds of green, and 2 pounds of straw opalescence for making the rose—which we find in opal, ruby, pink and

67

Millville

68

Millville

69

Millville
(Mold)

yellow. The yellow, incidentally, was a true canary yellow, and very expensive. The small amount used would indicate that this rose is scarce.

In the Barber roses, which have opalescent tips, the petals are never compact, but have a free and open appearance. Both the blossom and the leaves are in suspension slightly above the base. (See Illustration 67.) The Jersey roses, aside from the rare yellow specimens, are considered finest and most rare when the flower is accompanied by a bud and a real rose shaped leaf.

The Millville factory, of course, used a great many subjects other than the Jersey rose. Paperweights began to be made there about 1860. Early Millville weights such as Devil's Fire, Fountain, Remember Me (Illustration 68), and a lily were not impressive. With the establishment of the wooden mold department in 1863, however, the weights began to stand out as both unusual and attractive.

To return to the subject of the Jersey rose, it should be said that this subject was also dealt with in an interesting manner by all the workmen whose names are mentioned. In contrast with the weights attributed to Barber, there are Jersey roses with the petals tapering to a point at the base. These and others showing variation from the typical Barber treatment were probably made by other workmen or by the use of a new hand forged iron crimp. Many of the roses made by Emil Stanger have petals which are quite pointed at the tips.

All the Millville rose weights have a footed base which is large and firm and well proportioned to the ball, and the ball rests in a cup-shaped socket on either a single or double base. The pink rose with leaves and bud shown in Plate XVIII is on a double standard. This weight was made by Ralph Barber as a gift to his superintendent, Mr. Franklin Pierce, and it is one of the choicest and most unusual of the Barber weights.

In another example of the Jersey rose, the flower rests on the bottom and the weight has a thin, frosted base. It should be pointed out, however, that this is distinctly not true to the form of the earlier weights.

Another specimen has a deep pink rose with opalescent tips and dark green leaves. A stamen has the same color as the petals. A similar construction is found in a yellow rose which appeared about the same time. An old workman of the factory who was familiar with a wide range of the subjects said that he had never seen such a rose. He remarked, at the same time, that almost anything might turn up, since many items were never repeated and some of the crimps were experiments. It should be explained perhaps that the crimps were iron molds for

70

Crimps

Courtesy of Edmund W. Minns

making the rose. The white rose was the result of trying out a new crimp, and the opalescent glass used in the flower was made in the Millville factory. No leaves were ever added to it, however, because that would have required the use of expensive colored glass which was bought elsewhere. The weight was evidently an experiment and expenses were being held down.

It is not worth while, of course, to quibble over the circumstances under which a weight was made if the result is attractive and represents good workmanship.

Leaves were made separately by men over a Bunsen burner in the lamp room, where the small pieces could be shaped and reheated. The rose was formed from a quantity of molten glass which was marvered (or rolled) into cylindrical shape and flattened at one end. Then the amount of colored glass necessary to form the rose was reheated and placed against the base. The rose crimp was forced quickly into the clear glass, and the form was instantly withdrawn. The inside base of the crimp was covered with a thin layer of plaster. The purpose of this was to prevent the intense heat of the molten glass from melting the petals where they were soldered onto the base. Leaves were then added to make the rose appear full blown. The whole was then dipped again and shaped, and a base was formed as desired. In the finished weight, the rose appears much larger than it really is, on account of the magnifying qualities of the glass. A green rose without leaves and the calla lily are two rare types seldom found.

An hour or more was required to assemble the various parts into a finished weight, and thereafter the

71

Millville

72

Millville

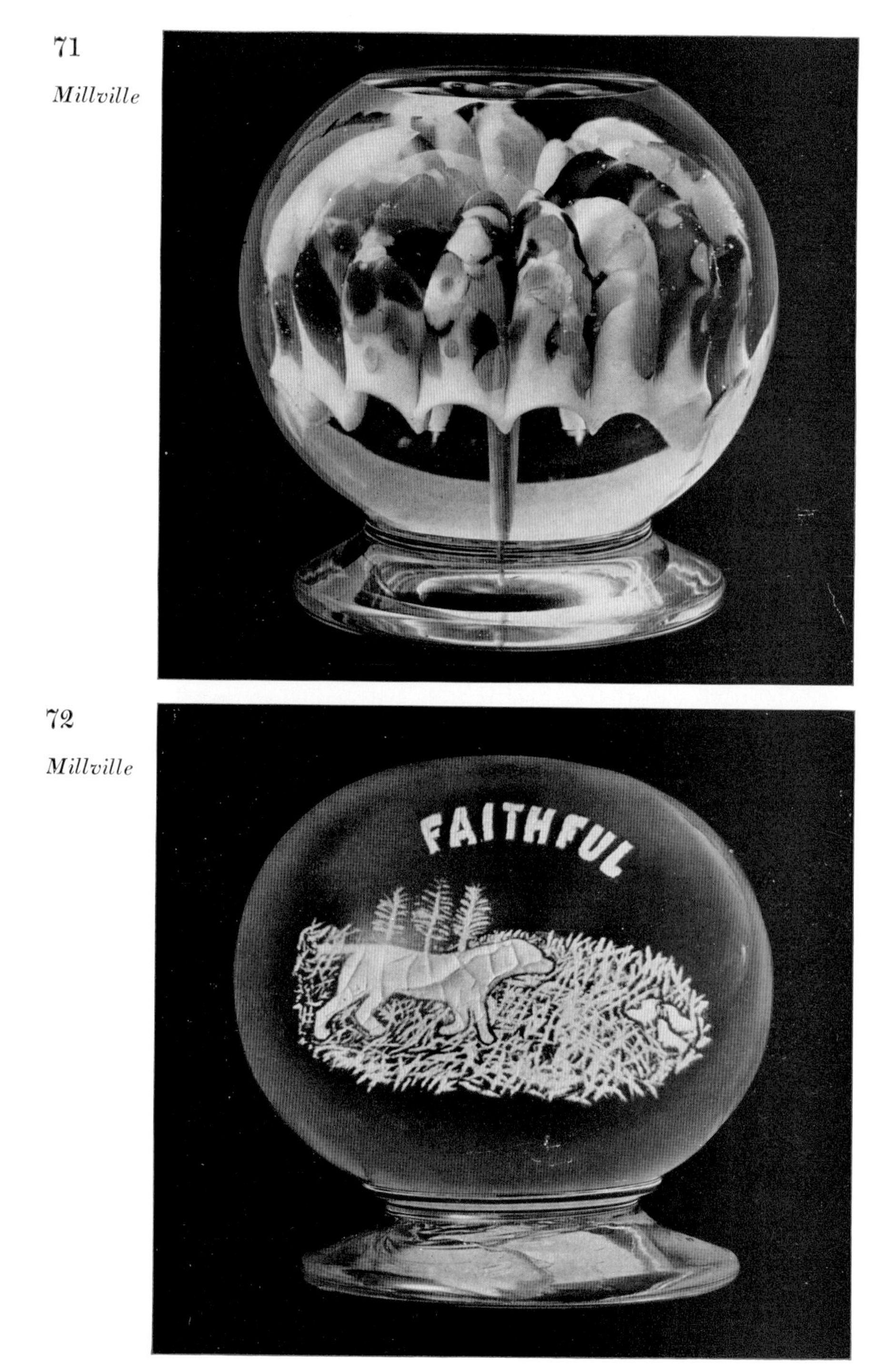

weight had to be tempered for three or four days in an annealing oven. The temperature in such an oven was maintained at 850 degrees to produce the temper that would enable the weight to resist a change of temperature or a heavy blow.

Ralph Barber, who made weights during the period from 1905 to 1912, died in 1936. In his later years he must have been greatly pleased to see his work so widely appreciated by collectors. No doubt he was also somewhat surprised to find that the weights which he made and sold for $1.50 each were being sought after eagerly at many times the small original price.

In paperweights of the mushroom or lily type, and in ink bottles, the crimp was pressed into the molten glass in a somewhat similar manner to the rose. The varied colored pieces of glass were placed on the flat end of the weight before the crimp was inserted and reheated. It was often necessary to repeat this process several times in order to collect more of the colored glass before finishing. A fine tool was inserted into the molten metal and quickly withdrawn in order to form the stem and bubble which are always found in these weights. In order to shape the pattern in the weight as desired, a small hook was run into the indentation. John Rhulander was accustomed to draw down the points of his weights with a hook, and this serves to make his work easily recognizable. (See Illustration 71.)

For the ink well, the glass was worked into shape in much the same manner, although it was not finished at the top or bottom. When the die and pontil rod were removed, it was blown to the shape desired. The stopper

73

Millville

was made in a similar manner, except that the neck was always shaped by hand. (See Illustration 73.)

Michael Kane, who came from Germany, made weights containing such subjects as the Faithful Dog (Illustration 72), Sail Boat (Illustration 74), and The Eagle. A mold of close grained fruit wood was used for forming the glass for such subjects. This was preferable because the heat was retained too long by the old iron molds. The wooden molds took the form of round wooden discs which might have a depression for the sail boat on one side, and for the eagle on the other. If it was necessary to use colored glass, a steel plate was cut in the machine shop. Having engraved the lines of the pattern in this steel plate, it was placed face up and the colored glass inserted into the pattern. Over this was placed a very thin piece of glass. It was important that the design be kept straight and that no air bubbles be allowed to mar the pattern. The plate was then carefully withdrawn, and the form was covered with more clear glass, and this was worked into proper shape with a wooden spatula. A foot was usually added to give the weight a better appearance. If examined carefully, the pieces of powdered glass can be seen in the patterns of weights made by this method.

The same process was used in fashioning the flat type of weight which shows a hunter in the field and a pointing dog. One difference in this type is that the outer crystal is always faceted. It seems that all the faceting of weights at Millville was done by a man named Clunn (Illustration 75.)

A pink water lily, with white and green encircling leaves and yellow stamen, was apparently made in an

74

Millville

75

Millville

iron mold. This type of weight was evidently not very popular, since specimens have become extremely rare. Weights were also made in which this lily is shown with all its stamens yellow, and other specimens show the lily entirely in white, suggesting that the latter was an early experiment (Plate XIX).

The pink tulip (Plate XX) which is about the same size as the Barber rose, and which has a yellow stamen and petals with fluted edges, is among the rarest of all the Millvilles.

There is also a well made deep red rose with very dark green leaves which recently appeared on the market. This rose sometimes shows more petals than the eleven or twelve which appeared in the older style. In the type of which we are speaking, the composition is modern.

The best article on the Millville weights was written by Mr. Edmund W. Minns which appeared in the November and December, 1938, numbers of *American Collector*.

John A. Gillerland

John A. Gillerland, having previously severed his connection with the firm of Fisher and Gillerland, built a factory for himself at Brooklyn, New York, in 1823. This he called the South Ferry Glass Works. Gillerland in his time was considered to be the best glass mixer in America, and he took the prize for his fine flint glass at the London Exhibition in 1851. The full significance of this award can be understood only when it is considered that his product was exhibited in competition with that of the ablest makers of flint-glass in both Europe and America.

Many of the good American faceted paperweights were

76

Gillerland

77

Gillerland

made in Gillerland's factory. The colors are clear and bright, and the workmanship is excellent. He excelled in the millefiori type, and it is probable that many of the fine millefiori weights which have been credited to other factories were really produced by Gillerland. One of Gillerland's finest things is a faceted paperweight with a bluish white overlay. This weight has an open design cutting on the crown, and the bull's eyes on the sides are typical of the product of this factory. The cutting on the remainder of the surface, however, is rather more intricate than that found on other specimens from this source. The interior of this weight has a high white opaque dome, with pink, light green, and white set-ups in the middle section, and dark blue set-ups around the lower rim. This is a strikingly heavy paperweight for its size, and the heaviness of the glass suggests its fine quality. The specimen referred to is shown in Illustration 76.

The second Gillerland weight chosen for reproduction (see Illustration 77) has a lacy background. A small cluster of flowers in the center bears some resemblance to certain floral subjects found in St. Louis weights. The outside rim has two circles, one of which is white, and the other alternating blue and yellow. The colors in this second weight are much stronger than in the first, although the blue set-ups are identical in both.

An arrangement employed by St. Louis, Baccarat, and Sandwich comprised a cluster of set-ups grouped to resemble flowers. In this design three or more set-ups were placed against three or more green leaves with a stem These were formed on clear glass, amber, or latticinio background, and sometimes there was an encircling row of set-ups around the outside rim of the weight. Some of these had plain crowns, others were beautifully faceted. The makers of weights of this type can easily be determined from the individual set-ups, and it may be said that the finest American examples were made by Gillerland.

A ceramic paperweight was made at the Gillerland factory which has in its center the single head of Queen Victoria, like the others which were made in the early years of her reign. On account of the remarkably close similarity of this head to another of Queen Victoria used in a Cambridge weight, one is tempted to speculate whether the two pieces were not produced by the same workman. Glass workers frequently change their allegiance from one factory to another, and it seems entirely probable that a Cambridge workman came to New York to repeat an earlier achievement in the Gillerland factory. Or, of course, the change may have been in the other direction—a Gillerland workman may have sought greater contentment in the green pastures of Cambridge.

Doerflinger

Christian Doerflinger, of Doerflinger & Sons, was born in Alsace-Lorraine in 1828. He came to America in 1841 and worked in two different factories in Brooklyn. In 1852 he opened his first factory on Concord Street but later established himself on Plymouth Street. Although the first output of this factory consisted of glass blanks, attention was turned later to the manufacture of glass for use in illumination, such as lamps, chimneys, and prisms. Eventually another Doerflinger factory was established at White Mills, Wayne County, Pennsyl-

PLATE XIX. *Millville*

PLATE XX. *Millville Tulip*

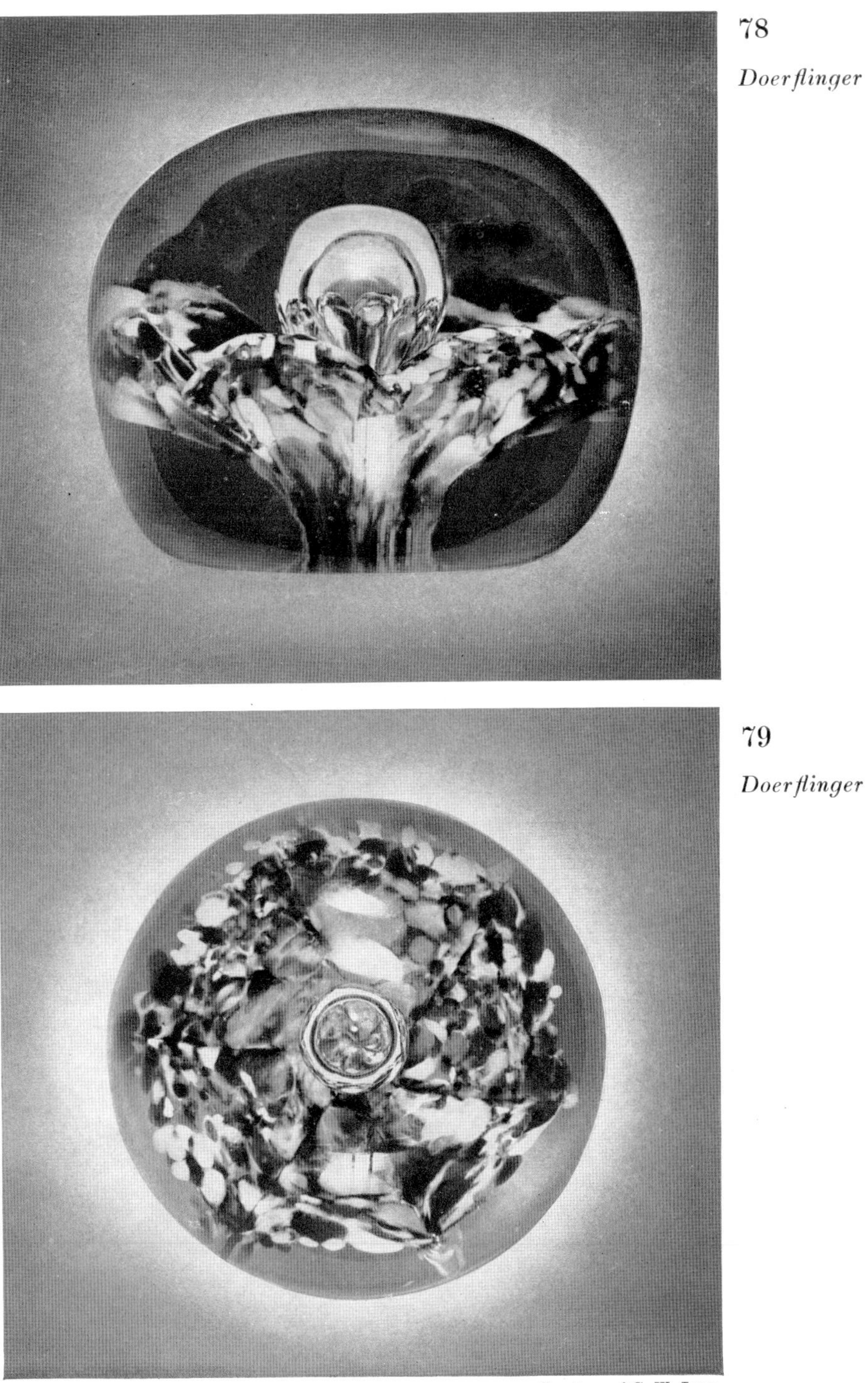

78

Doerflinger

79

Doerflinger

Courtesy of C. W. Lyon

vania, which engaged in the production of fine stem ware. In 1860 this factory received a large order of stem ware from Cuba to be engraved with the Cuban coat-of-arms. From 1880 to 1916 Doerflinger furnished the White House with its requirements of plate glass, the choice being made by the first lady of the land, and the engraving being done to her order. The flint glass produced in the Doerflinger factory was considered in its day to be among the finest made in America.

The custom of inscribing personal possessions, like plates, jewelry, and silverware with the name or initial of the owner is believed my many to be a modern idea. A little investigation shows that it is nothing of the sort. It was in vogue in the time of Queen Hatason in ancient Egypt, and descended to us through pagan, classical, and early Christian times. Far from being new, the practice belongs among the oldest customs of humankind.

80

Ink Stand Company

Ink Stand Company, Providence, Rhode Island

Every patriotic American will appreciate the old rock crystal weight which reproduces Plymouth Rock (Illustration 80). This piece was made by the Ink Stand Company, whose trade-mark indicates that it was founded in 1876. Molded on the face of this weight is the date 1620, the year in which the Pilgrims landed at Plymouth. The weight also reproduces the crack which was caused in Plymouth Rock by efforts to raise it in 1778. Around the outside base and rim is the following inscription, in letters so minute that they can be read only with the aid of a strong magnifying glass—

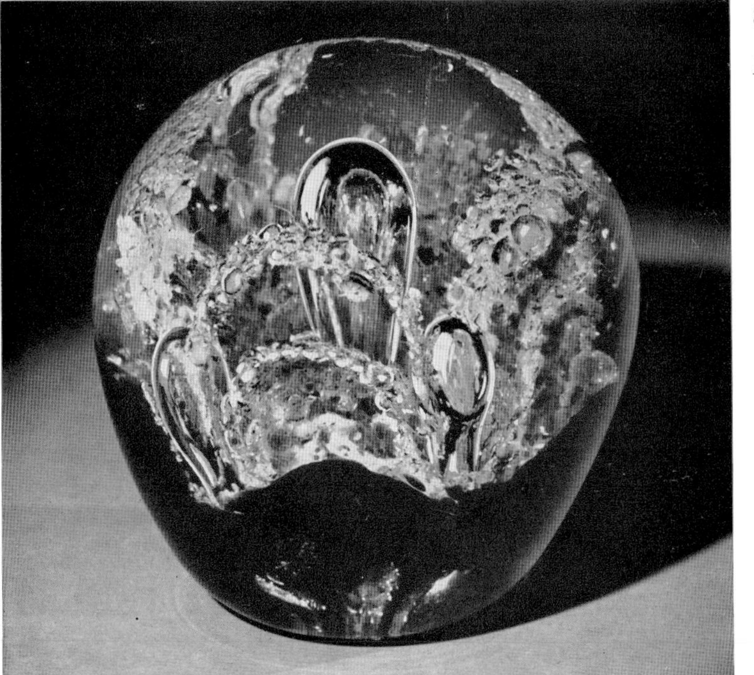

81

Fowlerton

"A Rock in the wilderness welcomes our Sires
From bondage far over the dark rolling sea,
On that Holy altar they kindled the fires
Which glow in our bosoms for thee."

The inscription further states that Mary Chilton was the first to land on Plymouth Rock, December 21, 1620.

Midwestern

Numerous glass factories sprang up in the Middle West when cheap fuel became available in this region with the discovery of natural gas. One of these was the F. B. Leach bottle factory established at Fowlerton, Indiana, in 1896. During the early period of this company's operation, until about 1898, it produced paperweights, glass hats, toothpick holders, and various other small articles. Thereafter—until the gas gave out in 1904—production was expanded to include fruit jars, glass oil containers, and bottles. The paperweights made by this company, mostly upright, bright designs, have been copied so successfully that it is difficult to distinguish the Fowlerton weights from later products.

Much quicksilver was used by the Fowlerton factory in fashioning its weights. One type combines arches of yellow and brown glass with mossy effects produced by the use of quicksilver. An elongated bubble forms the center. A large collection of these weights is owned by the Art Institute of Chicago. (See Illustration 81.)

Many other weights of which we have record were produced in factories throughout nearby Ohio. The White Glass Works of Zanesville used a rose similar to that of Barber in certain of its weights; but the weight and the rose were both flatter and smaller, and the rose had no leaves. From this source came also the only iris weight known in America.

The American lily weights, which are attractive in color, design, and workmanship, and are distinguishable by a tall center bubble were distributed in large quantities by the Ravenna Glass Company of Ohio about 1880. The originals had high crowns and were made large, somewhat like door stops. These are being copied extensively in smaller form today, and the copies can be picked up in any gift shop. A pair of mantel ornaments having a large center lily and three smaller ones arranged around the outside, all with large bubbles for stamens and all incased in a greenish white glass are fine examples of the work of this factory.

Although at least one glass factory was established in California as early as 1863, the greater part of the American glass industry did not show a great deal of inclination to follow the westward course of empire beyond the Middle West. Throughout the history of the world, important developments in glass manufacture have depended upon abundant supplies of good sand and cheap, suitable fuel.

* * *

It does not matter whether your collection of weights is large or small. You derive a certain amount of pleasure in possessing it, from learning the history of each piece, and from intimate contact with things that are beautiful. The interest increases with time, and the individual old glass paperweights carry with them the mystery and magic inherited from days long gone.

VII. PINCHBECK

PINCHBECK paperweights were made in England and France about the year 1850, and they were so called because each of them has at least a particle of the pinchbeck alloy in it somewhere.

All weights of this class require close study in order to appreciate their features, and to understand the reasons for the very substantial value which the best of them have come to have in the market for art objects.

The only glass in a pinchbeck weight is the thick flat glass over the top that envelops the picture. This glass extends beyond the base. Sometimes this protruding rim has been polished down to repair a nick that time has inflicted on its composition.

The pinchbeck weight is usually found to have a pewter base, although some are mounted upon a circular base of marble. It is supposed that the latter may have been made in France, since we know that the French weight makers used marble bases for their various products, including the snow weights. When marble bases are used, it will be found that these are firmly glued to the body of the weight. Pewter bases, on the other hand, are screwed to the glass, as can readily be seen in those cases where a portion of the pewter has been broken away from the glass.

The construction of pinchbeck weights was by no means an easy task, but required much skill and patience. The workman began by molding or sculpturing the pictorial subject which was to be enshrined in the glass. Then a cast had to be made in order to form the mold. The next step was to place over the mold a sheet of the pinchbeck gold; and this had to be burnished into the mold until the full design and all the delicate details had been worked out. Then it was lifted from the mold, and the reverse or finished side had to be subjected to such tooling and chasing as was required by the individual subject. It took a great deal of care and clever crafts-manship to avoid breaking or puncturing the thin sheet of metal, and to keep from stretching or distorting it in

82

Queen Victoria

any way. Inexpertness at any stage of fabricating the weight could easily ruin a design or bungle the construction.

One of the most interesting points to observe about the pinchbeck weights is that they are the product not of one art alone, but of several distinct arts. Combined in them is the work of the jeweler or chaser, the glass maker, and the miniature artist—each practicing an art which called for long experience and a high order of skill in itself.

What specific virtues and points of interest are worth noting in good examples of the pinchbeck weights?

As I write, I have before me a pinchbeck gold weight which contains a portrait of Queen Victoria (Illustration 82). The Queen is portrayed in natural colors, which are not laid flat upon the background but upon contours raised in high relief. The name "Victoria" appears in pinchbeck gold against a background of royal scarlet. This weight not only makes excellent use of the pinchbeck metal, but it incorporates a beautiful miniature painting as well. The entire composition is one of unusual charm and rarity.

Another of the pinchbeck class has a complete gold setting (Illustration 83). This gold is applied over a carved wooden mold, as in the former weights, but without a trace of any added color. They have the same form of glass on top and a pewter base which invariably is covered with red velvet, now worn by age, of the same style that appears sometimes on the smaller colored weights.

The gold subjects usually portray people, and some are even copies of noted paintings. The contour of these weights resembles a bit of fine Swiss carving, and as you closely examine one you are given the impression of a beautiful gold relief plaque.

So far as my experience extends, each of these weights is unique. I have never seen two alike, although this is not to say positively that duplicates may not occur. Their uniqueness, of course, goes far in accounting for their interest to collectors.

83

An All Gold Figure Paper-weight

GLOSSARY

BATCH. The mixture of raw material used for glass.

BLOWPIPE. A hollow rod used to inflate the glass object and attached opposite the pontil rod.

CANE. A long glass rod, plated layer upon layer in various colors.

CRADLE. The chair in which a glass maker sits to finish his work.

CULLET. Pieces of broken glass used by glass paperweight makers for the weights and also to add to the batch to replenish it.

DOUBLE OVERLAY. Two coatings of opaque enamel, first always white, next a color used on old weights before faceting.

FACETING. The various cuttings used by factories on the outside of a weight.

FLASH. A color applied by firing. Used in some of the Bohemian glass, but likely to wear off and not found in a good old weight.

GAFFER. The foreman or superintendent of a glass factory.

GALL. The scum taken from the melted glass after first boiling.

LATTICINIO. A decorative structure used originally by the Venetians and later by others in their paperweights. It was formed by the crossing and interlacing of delicate bands of white opaque glass.

LEHR (OR LEAR). An annealing furnace or oven for the glass.

MARVER. An iron table upon which the glass is rolled to make it smooth when taken from the oven.

METAL. The material used in the fusion of the glass.

OVERLAY. A colored coating of clear glass applied after weight is finished and before faceting.

PONTIL (puntee, ponty). A long solid iron rod used to hold the glass object being made.

PUNTY. A concave cutting which decreases the size of the encased pattern in a weight—in contrast to the convex form which increases the object. A weight with this kind of depression sometimes took the place of a wafer glass.

SET-UPS. The small pieces cut from a cane and used to form the patterns in a weight.

ACKNOWLEDGMENTS

IN sending this little book into the world, I wish to make grateful acknowledgment of the assistance generously given from many sources. Special thanks are due Mr. Charles Woolsey Lyon, whose invaluable cooperation has aided in the production of this book; also to Messrs. Alvin E. Bastien, W. Russell Button, Mildred Davison, Mrs. S. Edna Fletcher, and Edmund W. Minns. Among the sources consulted in the preparation of this volume were back files of such outstanding magazines as *Antiques, American Collector, Connoisseur,* and *Hobbies,* which contain considerable material bearing upon the subject, sometimes directly, sometimes indirectly. An article which appeared in *The American Mercury,* entitled "Glass Magic" by Mr. J. D. Ratcliff, was helpful in my brief discussion of Corning glass. Among the books referred to, either for information or verification of facts, the following were found most helpful: "Old Glass" by H. Hudson Moore; "Cambridge Glass" by Laura Woodside Watkins; "Antique Fakes and Reproductions" by Ruth Webb Lee; and "Five Thousand Years of Glass" by Frances Rogers and Alice Beard. "American Glass" by Mary Harrod Northend is a fine reference work on the general subject of antique glass, although it does not deal specifically with paperweights. "Early American Glass" by Rhea Mansfield Knittle contains invaluable information about the early factories.

INDEX